A BASIC BOOK FOR THOSE ENTERING ON THE PATH OF UNION WITH THE LIGHT.

LET RABBI BERG, A LIVING KABBALIST AND THE RAREST OF TEACHERS, OPEN THE DOOR TO YOUR SOUL AND SHOW YOU HOW TO REALLY KNOW YOURSELF.

WITH A SIMPLE, STRAIGHTFORWARD APPROACH, RABBI BERG DE-MYSTIFIES THE KABBALAH AND SHEDS LIGHT ON THE NATURE OF MAN AND HIS PLACE IN THE UNIVERSE.

HERE IS A UNIQUE SYNTHESIS OF COSMIC CONSCIOUSNESS AND THE WORLD OF THE FIVE SENSES.

KABBALAH CENTRE BOOKS

THE ZOHAR, *24 volumes. by Rabbi Shimon Bar Yohai, The cardinal work in the literature of Kabbalah — original Aramaic text with Hebrew translation and commentary by Rabbi Yehudah Ashlag.*

AN ENTRANCE TO THE TREE OF LIFE, compiled and edited by Rabbi Philip S. Berg (also available in Spanish)

AN ENTRANCE TO THE ZOHAR, compiled and edited by Rabbi Philip S. Berg

ASTROLOGY: THE STAR CONNECTION, Rabbi Philip S. Berg (also available in Hebrew, French, Spanish, Russian and Persian)

GENERAL PRINCIPLES OF KABBALAH, Rabbi M. Luzatto

GIFT OF THE BIBLE, Rabbi Yehudah Ashlag (also available in Hebrew)

KABBALAH FOR THE LAYMAN I, Rabbi Philip S. Berg (also available in Hebrew, Spanish, French, Russian, German, Persian, Chinese and Portuguese)

KABBALAH FOR THE LAYMAN II, III, Rabbi Philip S. Berg (also available in Hebrew, Spanish and French)

LIGHT OF REDEMPTION, by Rabbi Levi Krakovsky

POWER OF THE ALEPH BETH I, II, Rabbi Philip S. Berg (also available in Hebrew, French and Spanish)

REINCARNATION: WHEELS OF A SOUL, Rabbi Philip S. Berg (also available in Hebrew, Spanish, French, Russian and Persian)

TEN LUMINOUS EMANATIONS I, II, compiled and edited by Rabbi Philip S. Berg (also available in Hebrew)

THE KABBALAH CONNECTION, Rabbi Philip S. Berg (also available in Spanish)

TIME ZONES: YOUR KEY TO CONTROL, Rabbi Philip S. Berg (also available in French and Spanish)

TO THE POWER OF ONE, Rabbi Philip S. Berg (also available in Spanish and French)

ZOHAR: PARASHAT PINHAS, VOLS. I, II, III, translated, compiled and edited by Rabbi Philip S. Berg

---

SOON TO BE PUBLISHED

KABBALISTIC MEDITATION, Rabbi Philip S. Berg

TEN LUMINOUS EMANATIONS, VOL. III, IV compiled and edited by Rabbi P. S. Berg

TIME ZONES: YOUR KEY TO CONTROL, Rabbi Philip S. Berg, Russian and Persian Translations

ZOHAR: PARASHAT PINHAS, VOL. I, translated, compiled and edited by Rabbi Philip S. Berg, Spanish Translation

BOOKS AND TAPES AVAILABLE
AT BOOKSELLERS AND KABBALAH CENTRES AROUND THE WORLD

The Kabbalah Centre Books are published in English, Hebrew, French, Spanish, Russian, German, Portuguese, Persian and Chinese.

KABBALAH
FOR THE
LAYMAN

KABBALAH

VOLUME I

RESEARCH CENTER OF KABBALAH PRESS
JERUSALEM — NEW YORK

FOR THE

LAYMAN

A GUIDE TO EXPANDED CONSCIOUSNESS

RABBI PHILIP S. BERG

First Printing - June 1982
Second Printing - November 1982
Third Printing - March 1983
Fourth Printing - March 1984
Fifth Printing - August 1984
Sixth Printing - May 1985
Seventh Printing - November 1987
Eighth Printing - November 1988
Ninth Printing - February 1989
Tenth Printing - December 1991

REVISED EDITION
December 1991

ISBN 0-943688-00-0 (Hardcover)
ISBN 0-943688-01-9 (Softcover)

For further information, address:

RESEARCH CENTRE OF KABBALAH
200 PARK AVENUE, SUITE 303E
NEW YORK, N.Y. 10166

— or —

P.O. BOX 14168
THE OLD CITY, JERUSALEM

PRINTED IN U.S.A.

1991

*I would like
to express my grateful thanks for
the help and advice given to me by my wife,
Karen,
who patiently edited, criticized and typed
the manuscript. Without her
encouragement and faith,
this book might have remained just
another Leo dream.*

ABOUT THE AUTHOR

RABBI PHILIP S. BERG is Dean of the Research Centre of Kabbalah. Born in New York City, into a family descended from a long line of Rabbis, he is an ordained Orthodox Rabbi (from the renowned rabbinical seminary Torat VaDaat). While traveling to Israel in 1962, he met his Kabbalistic master, Rabbi Yehuda Zvi Brandwein, student of Rabbi Yehuda Ashlag Z"L and then Dean of the Research Centre of Kabbalah. During that period the Centre expanded substantially with the establishment of the United States branch in 1965 through which it currently disseminates and distributes its publications. Rabbi Berg did research at the Centre under the auspices of his beloved teacher Rabbi Brandwein Z"L, writing books on such topics as the origins of Kabbalah, creation, cosmic consciousness, energy, and the myths of the speed of light and the light barrier. Following the death of his master in 1969, Rabbi Berg assumed the position of Dean of the Centre, expanding its publication program through the translation of source material on the Kabbalah into English and other languages. Rabbi Berg moved with his devoted and dedicated wife Karen to Israel in 1971, where they opened the doors of the Centre to *all* seekers of self identity, establishing centres in all major cities throughout Israel, while at the same time lecturing at the City University of Tel Aviv. They returned to the United States in 1981 to further establish centres of learning in major cities all over the world. In addition to publishing scientific and popular articles, Rabbi Berg is the author, translator and/or editor of eighteen other books, including *Wheels of a Soul*, and *Time Zones* and *To the Power of One*.

ACKNOWLEDGEMENTS

I would like to express my gratitude to Roy Tarlow for compiling, reviewing, and editing the manuscript. He made fundamental and frequent contributions to the essential ideas and their connections to the overall style. The delight I found in our many discussions is one of my principal rewards from this book. Many heartfelt thanks to him for his helpful suggestions and careful proofreading of the manuscript. I would also like to express my warm appreciation to Osnat Youdkevitch for the artwork and the beautiful interior design.

To the spiritual growth of

S. PHILIP TARLOW

and through him to the Family

and through them to the World

and through them

to the

Universe

TABLE OF CONTENTS

*does not consume; the attachment of the blue or
black light to the physicality of the candle; the
wick, blue/black light and white light symbolizing the three columns of the Sfirot; the choice of
cutting ourselves off or connecting with the
Creator*

APPENDICES

ABOUT THE ZOHAR

The ZOHAR, the basic source of the Kabbalah was written by Rabbi Shimon bar Yohai while hiding from the Romans in a cave in Pe'quin for 13 years. It was later brought to light by Rabbi Moses de Leon in Spain and further revealed through the Safed Kabbalists and the Lurianic system of Kabbalah.

The programs of the Research Centre of Kabbalah have been established to provide opportunities for learning, teaching, research, and demonstration of specialized knowledge drawn from the ageless wisdom of the Zohar and the Jewish sages. Long kept from the masses, today this knowledge should be shared by all who seek to understand the deeper meaning of our Jewish heritage, a more profound meaning of life. Modern science is only beginning to discover what our sages veiled in symbolism. This knowledge is of a very practical nature and can be applied daily for the betterment of our lives and of humankind.

Our courses and materials deal with the Zoharic understanding of each weekly portion of the Torah. Every facet of Jewish life is covered and other dimensions, hitherto unknown, provide a deeper connection to a superior Reality. Three important beginning courses cover such aspects as: Time, Space and Motion; Reincarnation, Marriage, Divorce, Kabbalistic Meditation, Limitation of the five senses, Illusion-Reality, Four Phases, Male and Female, Death, Sleep, Dreams; Food: what is kosher and why; Circumcision, Redemption of the First Born, Shatnes, Shabbat.

Darkness cannot prevail in the presence of Light. A darkened room must respond even to the lighting of a candle. As we share this moment together we are beginning to witness, and indeed some of us are already participating in a people's revolution of enlightenment. The darkened clouds of strife and conflict will make their presence felt only as long as the Eternal Light remains concealed.

The Zohar now remains a final, if not the only, solution to infusing the cosmos with the revealed Light of the Force. The Zohar is not a book about religion. Rather, the Zohar is concerned with the relationship between the unseen forces of the cosmos, the Force, and the impact on Man.

The Zohar promises that with the ushering in of the Age of Aquarius the cosmos will become readily accessible to human understanding. It states that in the days of the Messiah "there will no longer be the necessity for one to request of his neighbor, teach me wisdom" (Zohar III, p.58a). "One day they will no longer teach every man his neighbor and every man his brother, saying know the Lord. For they shall all know Me, from the youngest to the oldest of them (Jeremiah 31:34).

We can and must regain control of our lives and environment. To achieve this objective the Zohar provides us with an opportunity to transcend the crushing weight of universal negativity.

The daily perusing of the Zohar, without any attempt at translation or "understanding" will fill our consciousness with the Light, improving our well-being and influencing all in our environment toward positive attitudes. Even the scanning of the Zohar by those unfamiliar with the Hebrew Aleph Beth will accomplish the same result.

The connection that we establish through scanning the Zohar is a connection and unity with the Light of the Lord. The letters, even if we do not consciously know Hebrew or Aramaic, are the channels through which the connection is made and could be likened to dialing the right telephone number, or typing in the right codes to run a computer program. The connection is established at the metaphysical level of our being and radiates into our physical plane of existence...but first there is the metaphysical "fixing". We have to consciously, through positive thoughts and actions, permit the immense power of the Zohar to radiate love, harmony and peace into our lives for us to share with all humanity and the universe.

As we enter the years ahead, the Zohar will continue to be a people's book, striking a sympathetic chord in the hearts and minds of those who long for peace, truth and relief from suffering. In the face of crises and catastrophe it has the ability to resolve agonizing human afflictions by restoring each individual's relationship with the Force.

INTRODUCTION

INTO THIS MYSTERIOUS UNIVERSE WE ARE BORN, WITH NO apparent set of instructions, no maps or equations, no signs or guideposts, nothing but our equally unfathomable instincts, intuitions, and reasoning abilities to tell us where we came from, why we are here and what we are supposed to do. What we do possess — perhaps the key to our survival as a species — is an almost unquenchable *need to know*. A human being comes into this world with a passionate sense of wonder and inquisitiveness and an equally powerful need for self expression. Yet, somehow, these seemingly indelible primal imperatives become eroded, as a rule, after only a few years' exposure to modern "reality" and contemporary educational methods.

While there can be no question that we, as a species, have established deep and penetrating channels into the how of things — indeed, it may be said that in some respects we have become masters of material existence — we have, however, made scant headway toward finding the source of the mighty river. Why? In spite of our many stunning scientific achievements, we remain today no closer to uncovering the answer to the ultimate questions as to the essence of existence than we were when First Man and First Woman gazed awe-struck into a clear, starry sky and contemplated the Great Mystery.

Who are we? Where did we come from? Why are we here? Why did the universe come into being? Did life on earth emerge as a matter of chance, or was it the conscious act of a Supreme Being? Is our suffering a cruel hoax or is it a constituent element of some grand design?

Despite all our best efforts to arrive at a conclusive understanding of reality, the essential questions concerning the nature of existence remain profoundly impenetrable. That, in itself, is not particularly alarming — what is to me unsettling is the fact that today, perhaps as in no other time in history, we, as individuals, are failing to meet the challenge to probe life's mysteries. No longer do we feel comfortable attempting to answer the essential questions. We have grown meek, surrendering the investigation, instead, to so-called specialists, consultants, experts, and professionals. To what do we owe this mass flight from meaningful inquiry and personal expression?

For too long — nearly three centuries — the struggle to probe the nature of existence and resolve life's apparent paradoxes has increasingly been considered the exclusive province of specialists. Questions as to the how of things we relinquish to the scientists, doctors, lawyers, engineers, analysts, and artisans. Why-related questions, such as those addressing themselves to the meaning of life, we leave on the doorstep of the philosophers, psychologists, artists, poets, and theologians. Well, as one may argue, this is, after all, the age of specialization. With so much knowledge in the world, so much information, how can the "common" person compete with the experts, with their advanced degrees, generous grants and banks of computers, while the common person must make do with seemingly obsolete equipment, reason, hunches, and raw instinct? The question, the Kabbalist will tell us, is not so much one of out-*thinking* the experts, but rather of simply out-*knowing* them.

Consider the following possibility (though, indeed, in the eyes of certain specialists, the very naming of it is undoubtedly deserving of no less than capital punishment): that the very framework on which the thinking of many so-called scientific authorities is based, the foundation of assumptions, the methods on which their theories and pronouncements have been so painstakingly fabricated, are not, as they would have us believe, infallible.

Could it be that the experts in whom we have placed our absolute faith and trust, have, in certain respects, been acting under a crude illusion? The continuing hostility and dissension among the ranks of specialists, authorities, and staunch defenders of so-called higher learning go a long way toward providing evidence in favor of this point of view. In fact, all that the experts can seem to agree on is that they vehemently disagree. Is it conceivable that the entire philosophical edifice upon which science is based is about to topple and that we, the "common man", might perhaps have made a large — even fatal — blunder by relinquishing to its practitioners our most precious gifts: our sense of wonder, our natural curiosity, our need for self-expression?

The Zohar's answers to these questions is emphatic in the affirmative. The scientific mind cannot now, and never will —

without undergoing a complete metamorphosis — get to the bottom of life's why-related mysteries, for the simple reason that the scientist's dominant how-to mode of consciousness is incapable of concocting anything but a how-related construct.

How did it happen? Why? What precisely caused Western man to surrender to others his inalienable right to probe life's most intractable mysteries? No single cause can be named. The reason cannot be pinned on any one source or blamed on any individual. However, if an inventory were to be compiled of people throughout the ages whose philosophies have profoundly affected, for better or for worse, the human psychological condition, the French mathematician and philosopher, René Descartes (1596-1650), would be high on the list.

René Descartes, the father of modern science, cooked up a theory, the leftovers of which are still being rehashed to this day. Descartes defined reality as consisting of only that which can be analyzed or explained by the scientific method. By this way of thinking, which is known as the Cartesian paradigm, the world is seen as an immense agglomeration of mass and motion, adhering to mathematical laws. Descartes' paradigm, which has remained the dominant framework of Western consciousness from the seventeenth century to the present, has proved itself to be an excellent tool for answering *how*-related questions, but it has done nothing with respect to answering those questions that are related to life's greatest mysteries, those based on the question, *why*?

Why was the world created? Why were we born? Why, in light of our incredible technological strides, our great achievements in medicine, science, psychology, and physics, do we remain in the dark as to the real meaning of our lives?

Unlike the Cartesian paradigm, the Zohar provides a framework for answering life's most profound and perplexing questions. Indeed, the perceptive reader will find in the Zohar satisfactory answers to all of the above questions and many more. Be forewarned, however, the solutions to life's great mysteries are not served up, so to speak, on a silver platter. Nor are they necessarily easily swallowed, digested, or assimilated. *Parashat Pinhas*, the trilogy of *Zoharic* texts, translated into English for the first time, is not, as the expression goes, "an easy read". Some paragraphs — indeed, some phrases and sentences — are so densely layered with meaning that the reader might quite literally experience dizziness and fatigue at trying to comprehend them.

Be advised in advance, then, that the *Zohar* is not for everyone. It will not be appreciated by those who are unyieldingly rational and pragmatic, or those who are so solidly imprisoned in the Cartesian paradigm that to attempt escape would be unthinkable — though both groups will certainly find here much to rail against! Those readers, however, who are eager to accept the challenge of grappling with life's most intransigent mysteries will, I believe, discover in the multilayered symbolism that makes up *Zoharic* reality all of the ways and means to do so, and will accordingly be rewarded beyond their happiest expectations.

The purpose of this book is not just to provide the reader with a taste of the vast world of Kabbalistic thought, but also to argue the necessity for each individual to return to the understanding of the universe and its law that is provided to us by the Kabbalah.

There is no doubt that the recent rebirth of interest in mysticism and the occult has given an important impetus to the resurgence of Kabbalah and it has come as a surprise and a revelation to many to discover within Judaism the unsuspected existence of a full-fledged complex and absorbing system — a system, furthermore, that can deal confidently with all the problems presented by existence in the twentieth century and beyond.

It is becoming increasingly clear that what is needed is the knowledge that will enable us to redefine such basic terms as Good and Evil for a generation to whom these terms have become meaningless, and help us make sense of a universe that now displays such opposites as space travel and drug addiction, high-tech computers and atomic destruction. Knowledge of Kabbalah leads one to a correct understanding of these problems, and provides the key to eventual mastery. Unfortunately, the widespread ignorance surrounding the nature and content of Kabbalah has led to the growth of false ideas, fear, and mistrust; those few Kabbalists in the past who misused their powers, or misinterpreted their role as the bearers of wisdom, have had a detrimental effect on the popular attitude towards Kabbalah that is quite disproportionate to their numbers. A clearer and more accurate position was taken by Rabbi Shimon bar Yohai, who made the vital distinction between Ta'amei Torah, the hidden understanding of the Torah that should be accessible to all who wish to learn, and Sitrei Torah, the secret teachings that should be accessible only to those who have reached the point where they can deal adequately with the power contained therein. In the years to come, with the increasing knowledge and understanding of Kabbalah, we shall witness a turning to the teachings of the *Zohar* by scientists to refine their knowledge of the essential structure and laws of the universe.

Part one

THE BODY
OF
KNOWLEDGE

Rabbi Hiya adduced here the verse:
"I was asleep but my heart was awakened,
it is the voice of my beloved that knocks,
saying Open to me, my sister ..." (S.S. 5:2).

Says the Community of Israel: I was asleep in the
captivity of Egypt, when my children were sore oppressed,
but my heart was awake to preserve them
so that they should not perish under the oppression.
"The voice of my beloved", the Holy One, blessed be He, saying:
Open to me an opening no bigger than the eye of a needle,
and I will open to thee the supernal gates.
"Open to me, my sister" because thou art the door through
which there is entrance to Me;
if thou openest not, I am closed.

Zohar III, P.95a

1

THE MAIN TEACHINGS

THE VASTNESS OF THE SCOPE AND QUANTITY OF KABBALISTIC literature should not prevent us from examining some of the main ideas and concepts in a concise form, bearing in mind at all times that such a shortening does have its limitations, and is chiefly intended for the newcomer to Kabbalah. In this task we are served well by Rabbi Ashlag, whose comprehensive works impose some order on the often complex and diffuse thoughts of the Zohar. It should be noted that the wisdom of the Kabbalah is anything but dogmatic; at all times it is left to the reader to make the choice of whether to believe or not, using the standards set down herein. Very little is left to supposition or suggestive thinking, the central aim always being clear understanding and comprehension.

THE CREATOR

> *All-inclusive and lacking nothing — the Desire to Impart — sharing without diminishing — creating the metaphysical atmosphere for drawing the forces and energies from above.*

Rabbi Ashlag, in his work on *The Study of the Ten Luminous Emanations*, states that finding a way to refer to the Creator is difficult since we have no concept of his Being. Consequently, in addition to "Lord", "*Elokim*", and "Creator", Kabbalistic teaching also refers to the emanation of His essence, namely Light, Energy, Light Force, or Force.

There is one premise in the whole of Kabbalah, and only one. This premise, from which every idea contained in Kabbalistic teaching evolved, is that the Lord is all-inclusive, and that He lacks nothing whatsoever. The immediate conclusion that we can draw from this statement is that He is good, since as we shall shortly demonstrate, all aspects of evil stem from the root of unfulfillment. We can see this in our own lives, where all our jealousies, anger and hatred are a result of desires for emotional or physical gratification that is not forthcoming.

Having said that the Lord is complete and therefore good, we can now go on to describe the attribute of sharing through which we are aware of His existence — His desire to share. This is an extension of His goodness and is described in the Kabbalah as the Light. We know from our experiences in this mundane world that sharing, or imparting, is an attribute of goodness. If we consider any object or person that we would call "good" we will realize that the essential quality that all "good" things have in common is that they give us something that we want. That "something" might be physical as in the case of a benefactor who gives us physical gifts, or it might be an experience that gives us pleasure. The aspect of fulfilling a part of our desires remains the constant common factor. We call this factor "positive energy", since the positive force is always the one that is complete and tends to fill areas of incompleteness, or negativity. This positive energy is also called the Desire to Impart, or the Desire to Share. The word Desire is used because it reminds us that there can be no sharing of something we do not possess; thus we could paraphrase the Desire to Impart in the form of a Want to Give, expressing the sublime principle that the whole of existence is sustained from moment to moment only by the continuous gift of life from the Creator, fulfilling our "want" or Desire so that we can "give" or Impart. This is the total of all that we can know or say about the Lord: that He is complete and lacks nothing, that He is good, that His attribute is sharing or imparting and that the manifestation of that desire is called positive energy.

It might be thought that sharing, which is the only aspect through which the Creator is made known to us, implies diminishing; our experience in this world is that after we have shared or given something we are left with less than before. In fact, this is often not the case, since sharing is the prerequisite for receiving. When we share, we create the metaphysical atmosphere for drawing down the forces and energies from above. Nonetheless, we can safely say that a bottle of water from which half the contents are poured into another receptacle will contain less after the transaction than before. Can we then say that the Creator is diminished, by His sharing with us? The bottle is inanimate, and, although it contains some small degree of the Desire to Receive — without which it could not exist —

it does not have the power to draw down metaphysical energy for itself; when it shares, therefore, it is diminished.

When we share, as we have said, we may appear to have lost something, but we differ from the inanimate order of existence in that our Desire to Receive is far greater and is even increased each time we share; thus our apparent loss in the physical world is balanced by a gain in metaphysical power. A second example we might consider is that of a candle, whose light can light an infinite number of other candles without being diminished. To be sure the candle itself will grow smaller the longer it burns, but this is merely the "body" or vehicle by which the light is transmitted; the light itself remains constant. This is because light does not belong to the four levels of existence — inanimate, vegetative, animate and human — but is, like electricity, a force and a source of energy. As such it has a very close affinity for pure metaphysical energy, which gives us an insight into the importance of light in ritual and celebration.

To summarize, we can say that the concepts of goodness, beneficence, positive energy, the Desire to Impart, Light, all-inclusiveness, total fulfillment, and the lack of the Desire to Receive, are all manifestations of one single concept, all interlocking and inseparable, and comprising in their totality the nature of the Creator.

THE FIRST STATE OF EXISTENCE — THE *EIN SOF*

> *In the Endless World: Creation governed by cause and effect — the unity of the Desires to Impart and to Receive — the total fulfillment of all souls.*

The Kabbalah teaches us that the first state of existence of which we can have any knowledge is the *Ein Sof*, the Endless World. As its name implies, this state is without beginning or end, and within it there are no manifestations of the concepts of time, space or motion. Thus when we talk of events taking place within the *Ein Sof* we should always bear in mind that these are merely distinctions we impose, and not discrete operations within the Endless World. It is only through the separation of existence into the modes of time, space and motion that we can bring our limited powers of understanding to bear on a problem, but the unfolding of the process of Creation in the *Ein Sof* is governed purely and solely by cause and effect, with no discernible extension or movement. The Ari says of this stage of Creation that "There were no distinguishable or discernible levels or grades."[1]

This phase of Creation is shrouded in mystery and remains beyond the grasp of human conception and understanding. In it, we find the coexistence of the Desires to Impart and to Receive, representing together a simple and absolute unity that transcends material expression and the limits of time, space, and motion in its diverse and multifaceted form. This state might be compared to the seed, which contains all future manifestations in potential form, but which remains in complete unity at its source. Only when it begins to unfold and become subject to temporal and physical limitations do the elemental differences of the seed reveal themselves as separate entities— root, trunk, branch, and leaf.

When the exalted light of the *Ein Sof*, the Desire to Impart, the positive or causative factor, had completely and perfectly filled all existence, the Desire to Receive emerged within the world of the Endless. As a result of its emergence, no soul remained unfulfilled in its respective Desire to Receive—no soul required additional correction or perfection. This was eternal bliss at the pinnacle of its glory. The souls bore no trace of defect, lack, or inferiority, no jealousy or hatred of one another, since each received complete and instant fulfillment from the Light of the Endless. Out of His great love of sharing — boundless love — comes the essence of the Creator Who ceaselessly bestows His beneficence, the symbol of His divine perfection, the Desire to Impart, in which lies the root of His endless bliss.

CREATION, *Yesh Me'Ayin*

> *The Thought of Creation — the creation of the vessel — the creation of the Desire to Receive — something from nothing, the primal union of cause and effect*

We have said that the Creator's attribute is sharing or imparting; however, there can be no sharing unless there is some agent that can receive. We should also note that the Creator's infinite Desire to Impart implies a desire to fulfill every possible grade and quality of desires to receive: whether there was a desire for health, wisdom, money or possessions, its fulfillment was contained in the original Desire to Impart. Here we have what the Kabbalah calls the Thought of Creation, the process by which the Creator's infinite Desire to Impart led to the creation of a vessel to receive His blessings. Although we talk of "a vessel" (or *Sfirah*), we must remember that, due to the infinite Desire to Impart, the vessel must also be considered in the aspect of an infinite number of vessels, each receiving its individual fulfillment from the Creator. The creation of this vessel, according to the Kabbalah, was the beginning and the end of Creation.

If all that existed was the Desire to Impart, then all that was created was the Desire to Receive. The Desire to Impart could not have been created itself, for the process of creation implies that something previously non-existent has been brought into existence; yet we have already stated that the essence of the Desire to Impart is that it is full and lacks nothing. It is therefore inconceivable that the Desire to Impart itself should be created, since, lacking nothing, existence must be one of its attributes. We find this explained in Nahmanides' commentary in the line from the morning prayer, "He forms the light, and He creates the darkness." The Ramban asks why two different words are used — "formed" and "created" — and concludes that the light (which, as we have said, indicates the force of positive energy) could not be created, since creation indicates prior incompleteness, and the light is always whole. Instead, it was "formed", meaning that it was molded and circumscribed so it could descend from the *Ein Sof.* The darkness, however, can be said to have been "created", since darkness is an indication of incompleteness, or negative energy, and of the Desire to Receive. As such, it was not present in any form whatever within the Creator, but was created as a totally new phenomenon.

The creation of this vessel called the Desire to Receive is therefore called, *"Yesh me'Ayin"*, meaning that something (*yesh*) was created from nothing (*ayin*). The nothing from which the Desire to Receive was created should under no circumstances be mistaken for such concepts as emptiness or blackness: it is simply a state of non- or pre-existence, devoid of any attribute.

We have now reached, in our description of the process of the Creation of the worlds, a stage at which the actual essence of Creation has already taken place. The Kabbalah justifies its claim that the creation of the vessel of receiving, the *Yesh me'Ayin*, was the whole of creation, on the grounds that all subsequent emanations and unfolding are essentially no more than the multiplying results of this primal union of cause (positive) and effect (negative).

It is precisely from this mystical "nothingness" (*ayin*), known in Kabbalah as the "hidden cause", that all manifestations unfold, whether in terrestrial or celestial worlds. Consequently, this "nothing" is in fact immeasurably more real than any other existence, since it is from this stage that the entire creation sprang. Creation from nothing actually typifies, and is the prime example of, the process of emanation (which presupposes a *source* of emanation) and indeed the very creative process itself, which, as we have mentioned, produces something new without involving the processes of logical thinking.

The relationship between the Creator, His beneficence, and the *Sfirot*, is comparable to that of the soul and the body, and that of the essence and the vessel that contains it, except that the soul and the body differ in nature from the Creator. The soul, while symbolizing the imparting aspect of the Creator, nevertheless has the same characteristic as the body — namely a Desire to Receive.

The idea of "nothingness" is not as complicated and mystical as it might seem at first sight: it is merely a convenient conceptual aid to encapsulate the idea of something that results from a thought, an effect that ensued after a prior motivating cause and which, having been non-existent, is considered as "something that emanated from nothingness". This idea is at the same time simple and profound: it states that there is no such thing as "nothingness", the world having been made from the Eternal Substance of the Desire to Receive. The Creation of the world was the radical formation of this substance into what we know as our world.

This basic insight helps us to understand the paradoxes that permeate the entire Kabbalah. It deals with the world as it actually is, revealing the true immutable substance of the universe, as opposed to the ever changing appearance and transforming nature of the lower levels of existence. Only the underlying truth abides, the real substance of the universe, as opposed to the physical substance that we can touch but which decays and fades as the Light in it dies. Viewed in its simplest form, the Desire to Receive therefore signifies Creation in its totality. As a result of the Creator's original Desire to Impart, which was the motivating factor behind the Creation of the Desire to Receive, there arose a new phenomenon — the Desire to Receive, which is said to have sprung from "nothing" to indicate the elemental characteristic of the Creator.

However, there are still many stages of emanation before we can see the eventual emergence of our physical universe.

SHUTTING OFF OF THE LIGHT

> *The requirements to complete the cycle of receiving and sharing — the vessel's arousal of the Desire to Impart (second stage of Creation) — the vessel's voluntary emptying of its light (third stage), resulting in the Desire to Receive*

Let us return to the original Thought of Creation, which, as we said, was to share the Creator's boundless blessings. If we consider this concept of sharing, or imparting, we shall see that it makes certain demands on the recipient. We know from our own experience that the mere mechanical act of giving is, in itself, unsatisfactory. We do not give advice to the trees, nor do we offer money to animals. Clearly there must be a Desire to Receive on the part of the recipient, a knowledge of what the gift entails and signifies, before we can say that we are truly giving.

This is true for all levels of giving and receiving. There can be no sharing or imparting unless the recipient both knows and wants what he or she is being offered. Penetrating even more deeply into the nature of sharing and receiving, we find that these two criteria of knowledge and desire imply a previous possession of that which is sought, and that we must have lost what we possessed before we can desire it.

Who desires food when one has enough to eat? Who desires wealth when one has all that money can buy? It is only after we have lost something that we can want it back; while we still possess it, that particular vessel (or Desire to Receive) is filled, and feels no sense of loss.

If the Thought of Creation was to create a Desire to Receive, as we have said, then the creation of the vessel in its initial form in the *Ein Sof* did not completely achieve this end. This vessel, which we refer to as *Yesh me'Ayin*, is completely and everlastingly filled with Light and therefore cannot experience any Desire to Receive in itself. Indeed, its structure is indistinguishable from the Light, which is the Desire to Impart. The arousal of this Desire to Impart by the vessel is called the second stage of Creation — "stage" being understood in the sense of cause and effect, not, we should remember, in terms of time.

There now exists a situation where the infinite number of vessels all desire to share with one another. This, however, is not possible because each is, at this stage, completely fulfilled. So sensitive are the vessels to one another's desire to share, however, that each one empties itself voluntarily of its light. This is the only way in which they can enable one another to share.

Now as soon as the vessel brings about this shutting off, it becomes empty. This is referred to as the third stage. This emptiness brings about the fourth and final stage of Creation, for here we find the completion of the original Thought of Creation.

Once the vessel becomes empty, it feels the lack of what it previously contained — the Light of Creation. Here, then, we find for the first time the criterion for the existence of the Desire to Receive.

This stage completes the world of Creation that is called the *Ein Sof*. In Rabbi Ashlag's commentary on the Tree of Life, we read: "This last grade in its complete perfection is found only in the Endless World, before the creation of all the worlds."[2]

BREAD OF SHAME

> *The fulfillment of the Desire to Receive (fourth stage) causes Bread of Shame — the restriction (voluntary shutting off of the Light) — the laws of the flow and transfer of metaphysical energy are established — the*

> *voluntary becomes involuntary in the physi-*
> *cal universe — free will in the physical*
> *universe — the need to balance desires to*
> *receive and impart*

Rabbi Ashlag goes on to describe the next step in the emanation of the lower worlds: "The perfect will to receive of the Endless World underwent a restriction, or *Tzimtzum*."[3]

This is explained as follows: since the Desire to Receive, which had been established in the *Ein Sof*, was now receiving the infinite beneficence of the Creator (fourth stage), there arose a feeling called Bread of Shame. The vessel is receiving continuously, but can do nothing in return inasmuch as the Creator, being whole and lacking nothing, has no Desire to Receive. The vessel feels Bread of Shame because it is unable to earn what it is receiving. Furthermore, it is no longer merely a passive recipient as it was in the second stage of the *Ein Sof* before the appearance of the Desire to Receive. Now it actively wants the Light that it lost in the third stage of Creation, but cannot take it due to its inability to offer anything in return. The metaphysical energy generated by this situation brings about the restriction, or *Tzimtzum*. It leads, by the principle of cause and effect, to a voluntary shutting off of the Light, so that it can redress the existing lack of balance.

The resultant emptiness and lack of light gives birth to the infinite desires to receive of the physical world, in which we are placed in an incomplete state so that we can eliminate the Bread of Shame by sharing with others who are also lacking, and in this way fulfill our own desires.

This is the reason for placing an unfulfilled Desire to Receive in man. The original Thought of Creation was only to impart the Creator's infinite blessings, but we must first learn how to construct the link between giving and taking by means of *mitzvot* and precepts before we can bring that Thought to completion. It should be noted that the arousal of Bread of Shame is very different from the arousal of the Desire to Impart in the *Ein Sof* or the emptying of the vessels. The concept of Bread of Shame comes into existence only after the evolution of the Desire to Receive, which was the last of the four stages of Creation in the *Ein Sof*. "The restriction of Light" occurred outside the Endless World, and, following this first restraint, the function of limiting became operative in all the worlds below it.[4]

Some might ask why this whole process is necessary: if the Creator is All-Powerful, as we have said, why could He not have created a vessel that would have a Desire to Receive without a Desire to Impart? Why was it necessary to bring us down to this mundane world of suffering and hardship? How can we, with our desire for the pleasures and luxuries of our physical existence, ever hope to achieve unification with the Creator? The answer to these questions lies in a closer study of the Creation and a deeper understanding of the significance of the teachings of Kabbalah. To those who have understood the explanation given here it should be clear that the intention of the Creator was only to do good, this being His very nature. The restriction and emptying of the vessel in the fourth stage of Creation, however, was a voluntary act brought about by the vessel itself. The laws regarding the flow and transfer of metaphysical energy, from which all physical manifestations grow, were established from the beginning of Creation and are an expression of the attributes of the Creator. However, what is established by voluntary means on a high level becomes involuntary on successively lower levels. This is similar to a law which is established voluntarily by a process of debate and decision in the governing body of a state or country and which subsequently becomes binding on all the citizens over whom the jurisdiction extends.

The essential laws regarding the flow of energy in the universe were therefore established in the process of Creation. These laws include the reasons why we are present in this physical world, and why we are subject to the desires that we experience. Unfortunately, we are prone to forget that that which is voluntary in the *Ein Sof* becomes involuntary in our universe. The freedom that our souls chose voluntarily by restricting the Light of the *Ein Sof* was intended to give us the opportunity to redress the imbalance between what we were receiving and what we could impart to others. Nonetheless that freedom is still subject to the higher laws of Creation. While we can now exercise our Desire to Receive for our own gratification, without any thought of sharing with others, the essential structure of the universe (Bread of Shame, restriction) still applies. Gratification, whether it be spiritual or physical, will still last only if there is a balance between receiving and sharing.

This should answer the often-asked question regarding free will. Why couldn't the Creator merely have commanded us to obey the laws and precepts, instead of leaving us with such a confusing amount of choice? From what we have already said regarding the evolution of the universe, it should be clear that the decision not to receive was ours and ours alone. It was taken because of the imbalance that existed, and it was taken with the sole purpose of restoring balance. If the Creator were to order us to receive His infinite blessings, we would be faced with the same unacceptable imbalance that brought about the original feeling of Bread of Shame, which would in turn bring about a restriction, returning us full circle to our present state.

Clearly, our first concern should be to eliminate the feeling of Bread of Shame, for this is the cause of the restriction that cuts us off from the Light. Furthermore, it is as a direct result of the restriction that was brought about by the vessel of receiving that the forces of evil became manifest in our universe. Until there was a lack or emptiness there could be no evil, since the nature of evil is the unfulfilled Desire to Receive. If we examine our desires for the physical benefits of this world, we find that they all stem from this same root — the lack of fulfillment. Whether our desire is for money, status, or possessions, the common element is always the Desire to Receive, an awareness that we have lost a fulfillment we once had and can regain it by amassing physical objects. We have lost sight of the true purpose of our existence on this physical level so that the Desire to Receive is directed toward things other than the Light, which is the Desire to Impart. In showing us the forces by which the universe was created, the Zohar provides us with the reasons for our existence, and indicates unequivocally the work we have to accomplish during our brief period of existence in this world.

PURPOSE OF CREATION

Fulfilling mankind's created Desire to Receive

The question of the Creator's purpose is discussed by the sages of the Zohar who provide the simple answer that He might bestow upon it His infinite love and abundance. The thought behind Creation was to share with mankind. The effect of this motivating cause was the creation of man as a vessel for that bestowal, thus revealing the true essence of man as the Desire to Receive. Without this Desire to Receive, the creation of the world could not have proceeded, since the concept of positive energy must, out of necessity, come before the concept of negative energy; one could not possibly desire something without the prior capacity to desire.

Consequently we cannot speak of Creation when referring to the Light, which would designate something newly made or revealed. Creation refers not to the Light but to the newly revealed phenomenon of the Desire to Receive. Within this concept alone were contained all future manifestations of Creation, including the physical world together with its central point, Man.

At the time of the revelation of Creation, the Desire to Receive was like the seed of a tree. A tree is made up of roots, trunk, branches and leaves, all evolving indisputably from the seed, yet not discernable to the naked eye. While containing the future tree, the seed gives no sign yet of its future development into that tree.

Through a series of evolutions, man developed from his root or seed, which was the original revelation of the Desire to Receive. As man appears in our world, he is but an emanation or evolution of that Desire. His inner, hidden essence remains the Desire to Receive.

Now it should be clearly understood that this Desire to Receive is not necessarily degrading, nor is it to be considered a liability. On the contrary, as we have seen, it is the vital pivot of Creation. We can modify our Desire to Receive and channel its demands into areas that will strengthen us and draw us nearer to the Light, but we can never destroy it.

Only through a complete understanding of the Desire to Receive in all its manifestations will we come to a better understanding of our inner motivating consciousness and its relationship with our physical actions, and more importantly, a better understanding of our relationship with everyone we meet along life's road. All this information is provided for us by the Zohar. The Zohar shows us the sublime wisdom concerning the metaphysical characteristics of all Creation.

2

THE METHODOLOGY OF KABBALAH

HOW SHALL I KNOW? (Science and Kabbalah)

The quest for wisdom by Science — the interrelated systems of the physical and spiritual seen by the Kabbalah — the Zohar's emphasis on the role of man as a causative factor — the necessity to bridge the gap between the physical world of "How?" and the spiritual world of "Why?"— the coincidences of the world of appearance and the world of essence — the principle of harmony between branch and root

CONTEMPORARY MODELS OF METHODOLOGY STEM FOR THE most part from one or another of the many branches of science and technology, where increasingly sophisticated and complex techniques are being invented for the gathering and analysis of information; yet the farther science progresses down its chosen path, the more its methods seem to hinder its objectives. Today we have reached a stage where the language and terminology of the scientist are incomprehensible to the layman, and often to scientists in other fields as well. The scientist-philosopher of earlier generations who understood how his area of study fit in with the structure of the universe has given way to the special-ist, who limits his field of view in the vain hope of being able to master some small corner of the physical world. The hope is in vain, according to the teachings of the Kabbalah, because the physical world to which science has restricted itself is a world of effects. The true causes lay beyond it in the realm of the metaphysical. The fundamentals on which science relies cannot be substantiated without recourse to knowledge of higher non-physical modes of existence.

Even within these self-imposed restrictions, there are limits to the scope of the scientific method. On its own, it is incapa-ble of generating new ideas. Max Planck, the renowned physicist, wrote in his autobiography: "When the pioneer in science sends forth the groping fingers of his thoughts, he must have a vivid, intuitive imagination, for new ideas are not generated by deduction, but by an artistically creative imagina-tion."[5]

Without the subjective element of imagination, then, the objectives of science cannot be reached. But how "scientific" can science be if it depends on an impetus which, by its very definition, is unscientific?

The question is, perhaps, unfair; we are too ready to categorize ideas and principles, often forgetting that our categories are arbitrarily selected. Thus we think of science as dealing with knowledge, as its etymological root might suggest, and religion or philosophy as being concerned with truth or essence. The reality is not so cut-and-dried. And we find that all these disciplines attempt to arrive at a balanced combination of knowledge and truth together. This combination is the wisdom referred to by the sages as "seeing the consequences of action."

At the basis of this quest for wisdom lies the question of method: "How shall I know?" It is at this point that many feel that science and religion part company; thus, it is the claim of many modern thinkers that the advances in science are a direct result of the decline of religion as a force in the world. A Kabbalistic interpretation of history would challenge this assumption on the grounds that the implied distinction between knowledge and faith, together with the implied superiority of the former over the latter, is altogether false.

Contemporary scientific thought and writing on the subject of the scientific method show clearly that it is not the all-powerful tool that was once hoped. Perception, psychologists have finally realized, is an active process of sorting and interpreting, and not the passive, "objective" absorption of stimuli implied by the scientific method.

We must, in other words, have *a priori* knowledge — a concept that comes very close to the idea of faith — before we can see and understand. In the Kabbalah, there is no rigid distinction between physical and spiritual forms, and the picture presented is one of a total, unified, interrelated system. The *a priori* knowledge that casts doubt on the objectivity of science appears here in the form of the Desire to Receive, which produces a tendency to project onto "reality" what we want to see, rather than what might actually exist. This distinction between the outward appearance of physical bodies and their essence lies at the root of the difference of approach between science and Kabbalah. Science asks only how something exists within the dimensions or limitations of time, space, motion and causality; Kabbalah goes further and confronts the question of why things exist at all.

Having made this point, it should be said that increasingly modern science is coming to the realization that there are interesting and profitable areas of study that are not governed by the laws of time, space and motion. Instead of the observation of interactions supported by formulae and equations, the emphasis is shifting to the study of subtle and indefinable changes, so small that they may not follow the accepted behavior of the physical world. Perhaps, after all, physical reality no longer represents the final word in scientific disclosure.

The interpretation of the universe to be found in the Zohar stresses not only the polarities of existence — time and timelessness, motion and motionlessness — but also the role played by man himself as a causative factor. Here we find a description of true science by including the vital link played by man in the chain of discovery that stretches from the potential of knowledge in the universe down to its manifestation on earth. In this view, the scientist is as much a part of the universe as his discovery; indeed, he is a part of what he discovers, since he acts as a channel for the knowledge of his discovery. Thus we can no longer ignore the psyche of the scientist, the searcher after wisdom, and must take this additional variable into consideration when approaching theoretical physical phenomena. The question remains, is it possible to reach the ultimate goal of absolute truth, and if it is, how does one set about it?

We see an apple seed being planted and we assume that an apple tree, and eventually its fruit, will appear in due course, consistent with the law of cause and effect. Similarly in the realm of metaphysics, the delicate interplay of cause and effect is at work undetected by any physical means. The Kabbalah reveals this interplay by means of its explanations of the precepts, laws, commandments, prohibitions, allegories and tales of the Torah and Talmud. It is here we learn that the outcome and consequences of man's thought and actions are expressed in metaphors of reward and punishment. The Kabbalah reveals the mystical interpretation of the Torah's use of retribution, atonement, and suffering.

The function of this knowledge is radically different from that of science; it allows us to recognize the paths by which all creative processes emanate from the Light Force, the root of all Creation. Although the interaction of unknown elements may at times be revealed to the scientists, the essence of those elements which create the interactions is nevertheless completely obscured from our five senses. The strings of formulae and equations may describe the interactions — the effects — but these tools can never reveal the innermost secrets of the reasons for the reaction.

It is the objective of Kabbalah, especially in its current state of development, to provide the bridges and connections between the physical world of "How?" and the spiritual world of "Why?"

The language of Kabbalah is the language of man; it permits us to appreciate its profound wisdom to the utmost extent of our capabilities. To a generation that has witnessed innumerable advances in the atomic and subatomic fields of scientific research, the wisdom of Kabbalah can no longer be considered too remote or inaccessible; on the contrary, its most important teachings are becoming increasingly vital to maintain stability and harmony in a confusing technological world.

We come now to another area of difference between science and Kabbalah, an area which in itself suggests why many people believe Kabbalah to be even more complicated and inaccessible than science. The area of difference may be understood by considering the relationships that exist between objects. When we can see no connection between two objects or events, we say that they are unrelated, that their occurrence or presence together is coincidental. The root meaning of this word "coincidental", however, has quite the opposite meaning — it implies that our two events have occurred together. The teachings of Kabbalah indicate that the second sense, apart from being literal, is also the true one since two events that occur together, in whatever dimension (time, space, thought, etc.), are related to one another. The question now arises as to how this difference in interpretation arose. The answer is that science, however deeply it penetrates into the world of the senses, is still dealing only with external phenomena. It is the task of the scientist to examine and report on the outer surface, whereas the Kabbalist is concerned with pointing out the alignments (coincidences) of the world of appearances and the world of essence.

It is the objective of the Kabbalist to reveal the nature of the force of the Desire to Receive and the ways in which it is connected with the material world, and in addition to emphasize that there is no separation between the two worlds of essence and material existence. Here, however, there is an obvious dilemma, since the world of essence is described in the Zohar as being without form and cannot therefore be described physically. This is the *Sod* (secret) of truth: the Essence is never-changing, as compared with relative existence which is ever-changing. We can more easily understand this concept if we imagine curtains or veils of various colors placed between us and the sun; what we see is a change in the appearance of the light as it is filtered through the different colored curtains, but clearly, the actual light of the sun does not change. The essence of anything without form remains beyond the grasp of rational thought, and as such cannot be communicated through ordinary language. Only after it is interwoven with the external world of material existence can it be perceived, although even then it remains elusive and deceptive.

Mysticism relates to that which is without form. The sublime wisdom of the Kabbalah attempts to provide us with an understanding of essence and truth as a means of reaching a clearer perspective of our actions. Once we have achieved an understanding of the root or essence of any element, the subsequent interactions resulting from these basic elements will, of necessity, behave within the limits of the root, according to the principle that the branch (effect or interaction) and the root (cause) will always be in harmony. With this knowledge of essence we can avoid many of the conflicting and opposing viewpoints that hinder our progress and understanding, both as individuals and as nations.

Within the esoteric teachings of the Kabbalah, we set foot on that road of the essence, the root from which point of view alone we can see the straight and narrow path that leads to the Absolute. Once we recognize the realm of the real, where the veils of the material world are stripped away, we achieve universal oneness; having unveiled the mysteries and enigmas of life, we reach total truth. Hence the names *Wisdom of the Mysterious* and *Wisdom of the Truth* have been given to the

Zohar to denote the motif of this great work, the treasury of the Jewish mystical world of ideas.

This, then, is the distinction between science and Kabbalah. Even though both claim to be searching for truth, their expectations and criteria — and therefore their findings — are different. Kabbalah posits the existence of two basic levels of life — spiritual and material — and treats them both as proper subjects of investigation and analysis. It suggests too that, rather than being separate, there are strong and necessary links between the two, and that the Desire to Receive acts as a common link. The results of the Desire to Receive can, of course, be seen in the external world of appearances to which science has chosen to limit itself. However, the desire itself cannot be observed scientifically, since the world of the scientist — whether dealing with astronomy or subatomic physics — is one of outward effects, the prime causes always remaining hidden. To rely on the findings of science alone is tacitly to accept the view that the external world is self-contained and self-constructed, yet the further we delve into the mysteries of the physical universe, the more we become aware that such an interpretation just does not fit the information we now have at our disposal. The Kabbalah presents an alternative view to this mechanistic philosophy of existence, one that sees man as the ultimate missing link between the upper and lower worlds. That link, technically speaking, is in our very blood, which contains not only material substances but also the lowest spiritual level of the Desire to Receive — as it is written: "*haDam hu haNefesh*"[6], "the blood is the soul".

With its central core of symbolism, the Zohar reveals the essence of *Nistar* (the hidden) as tireless, changeless, motionless and eternal. Material phenomena are perceived by our physical channels of perception, while that which is beyond the range of our senses can be observed in part only through its interaction. Since each individual will make his or her own interpretation of his or her perceptions, these observed interactions of material phenomena may be understood differently among individuals.

CONDITIONS FOR STUDYING KABBALAH

> *Sitrei Torah and Ta'amei Torah — traditional prohibitions, regarding the study of Kabbalah applicable only to Sitrei Torah*

The claims made in this work for the study of Kabbalah are admittedly large; indeed, it is hard to imagine larger. This is because Kabbalah deals with ultimate reality, the ultimate truth of man's essence, and so no claim can be too great. On the other hand, the very power generated by this knowledge suggests that it would be wiser to restrict its availability to those who would best be able to handle it. It is therefore necessary to remind ourselves of the divisions and scope of Kabbalah.

Traditionally the study of the Kabbalah has been divided into two parts: *Sitrei Torah* and *Ta'amei Torah*. *Sitrei Torah* deals with Divine mysteries on the subtlest level and, as we have learned in dealing with the subtlest levels of manifest existence — the atom and its subatomic particles — there is serious danger at that level. Consequently this volume does not include the subject of *Sitrei Torah*.

Kabbalists such as Rabbi Shimon bar Yohai, Moses Cordovero, Isaac Luria, and many others in days past who possessed the secrets of *Sitrei Torah* were capable of transcend-

ing the physical realm altogether. It was through the power of
Sitrei Torah that many of the legendary incidents in their lives
occurred.

However, the study of *Ta'amei Torah* is not only possible
but is encouraged by the sages. *Ta'amei Torah* deals with the
order and purpose of Creation and leads to the very root of
one's existence and being. The traditional prohibitions against
the study of *Sitrei Torah* should not be carried over to *Ta'amei
Torah*. There is no place in Torah for the suppression of
inquiry and knowledge.

THE BIBLICAL METHODS OF KABBALAH

> *Transforming the Divine word into the
> limited language of Man — tales and para-
> bles of the Torah as symbols of the Divine
> mysteries — the essence of spirituality re-
> veals itself clothed in corporeal garments*

Though Kabbalah often deals with profound matters, it does
so in language that can be easily understood, a process which
in itself contains an important lesson. The method of dissemina-
tion of knowledge in the Kabbalah points to one of its central
teachings, namely that the Divine word of infinity can be
transformed into the finite and limited language of man.

This method is not exclusive to the Kabbalah. Its roots are
to be found in earlier written texts, particularly in those of
Mishnah, and even earlier in the writing of the Torah itself.
Both of these contain not only directives and imperatives but
also, perhaps less expectedly, stories, songs, parables and

histories, which would seem at first to have no logical place in such works.

For the Kabbalists, the stories of the Torah are merely her covering, under which exalted mysteries are concealed. They are only the garment for the body of the inner meaning. The Kabbalah seeks to imbue the commandments and laws of the Torah with their true, hidden spirit. Indeed, in the view of the Zohar, the tales and parables of the Torah are symbolic reflections of the inner metaphysical realm through which one could perceive the hidden divine mysteries of our universe.

Rabbi Shimon berates those who take these simple tales as relating only to incidents in the lives of individuals or nations.

Rabbi Shimon said:

> Woe unto the man who says that Torah merely presents narratives and mundane matters. For,if it is the nature of the Torah that it deals only with simple matters, we, in our day, could compile a superior version; if the Torah came just to inform us of everyday things, then the books now in the possession of the rulers of the world are of greater quality, and from these we could copy and compose a Torah. However, the uniqueness of the Torah lies in the fact that each word contains supernal matters and profound secrets.

> See how precisely balanced are the upper and lower worlds; Israel here below is the equivalent of the angels above, about whom it is written, "Who maketh His angels into winds" (Psalms 104:4). When the angels descend, they clothe themselves in earthly garments, without which they could not exist in this

world, nor could the world bear to co-exist with them if they were not thus clothed. If this is so with angels, then how much more must it be true of the Torah — the Torah that created them, that created all the Worlds through which all are sustained? The world could not endure the Torah had she not clothed herself in the garments of this world (tales and narratives).

Tales related in the Torah are merely the Torah's outer garments. One who considers the outer garments as the Torah itself, and no more, is a simpleton, and will not merit a portion in the World to Come. King David said, "Open my eyes, that I may behold wondrous things from your Torah" (Psalms 119:18), the meaning of which is that one should perceive that which lies beneath the outer garment of the Torah.

The clothes that man wears are the most visible part of him; senseless people, on seeing a well-dressed man, do not see any further, and judge him simply on the basis of his beautiful clothes. But in truth the pride of the garments is the body of the man and the pride of the body is the soul.

So it is with the Torah; its narrations relating to the mundane things of this world are but the garments which clothe the body of the Torah; the body of the Torah consists of its *Mitzvot* (precepts). Foolish people see the outer garment, the narrations of the Torah, and ignore that which lies beneath this outer garment. Those who understand more see the body beneath the garment, but the truly wise, those who serve the supernal King and who stood on Mount

Sinai, will penetrate to the soul of the Torah which
is its essence.[7]

When Rabbi Shimon says, "When the angels descend, they
enclothe themselves in earthly garments..." (above), he reveals
two significant *Sodot* (secrets) in relation to the conceptual
reality of mysticism. Spirituality, indicated in the Zohar by the
term "angels", cannot reveal anything of its essence unless it is
clothed in a corporeal garment. It is only when it is thus
clothed that the outward actions and interactions reveal, through
the five senses, something of their essence. It is largely through
these five senses that we develop the formulae and exploratory
devices that enable us to evaluate and store data relating to the
external world. The thoughts of man, before being put into the
corporeal garment of speech, remain hidden within the mind of
the individual. As a thought is revealed through this corporeal
garment of speech, a strange phenomenon takes place, in relation to both the speaker and the listener. The original thought
or idea in the mind may emerge in quite a different sense,
when it is passed through the "filter" of speech. Nor will the
words reaching the ears of the listener necessarily correspond
to those uttered by the speaker. Indeed, it is remarkable how
many divergent points of view can arise among a number of
listeners from an idea expressed by one individual. Taken one
step further, we might pass a voice through the medium of a
telephone or taperecorder, whereupon the resulting distortion
will often appear to the original speaker to be the voice of
someone else; thus we see how misleading the forms of the
mundane world can be.

However, cautions Rabbi Shimon, without these earthly
garments — the cables and vessels — metaphysical essence
could not co-exist with, or be observed by, this world; this is
why the Zohar concerns itself with the study of essence,

providing instant understanding of its characteristics, and thereby avoiding the potential inaccuracies and misinterpretations that inevitably arise from the study of the earthly garments of action and interaction.

This, then, is the first *Sod* revealed by Rabbi Shimon: that metaphysical concepts and essence are, and must be clothed in corporeal garments, and all actions and interactions that we observe consist of, and are governed by, metaphysical forces.

Now to the second *Sod* contained in this passage of the Zohar, which appears in the section, "nor could the world bear to co-exist with them if they were not thus clothed." To explain this subtle but penetrating secret, let us consider the case of electricity. We know that electrical current is an energy force that must be contained within some sort of cable for it to be useful. In the case of a fallen power line or a broken cable, there is the danger of electric shock or fire, since the flowing current is no longer contained, and anything with which it comes into contact will be unable to contain this naked energy. Within the metaphysical realm, the pattern is identical: there is a great danger here when an imbalance exists between imparting positive forces and receiving negative forces. The overloading of an electrical cable (the overtraining of an individual's mental capacities) signals trouble, since the receptacle or vessel simply lacks the insulation and safeguards for the directed output of energy (the flow of ideas). These analogies are relevant at the peripheral areas of the pure essence of spirituality. How much greater, then, is the need for a suitable medium or garment to transmit the omnipotent beneficence and sublime esoteric wisdom of metaphysics!

The Zohar, interwoven with profound philosophic views, reveals that the biblical narratives are the vehicles by which the

Divine mysteries of our universe can be understood. Furthermore, through a system of laws and commandments, which act as a garment for true spirituality, the same objective is achieved — as is seen in the beauty of spiritual meditation clothed in a garment of systemized prayer, or in the holiness of the Sabbath, when its metaphysical implications are fully understood.

The question of how we can be certain of the interpretation of the metaphysical plane that is revealed by the Zohar is carefully considered by its author. "And for those persons who do not know, yet have a desire to understand," declares the Zohar, "reflect upon that which is revealed and made manifest (in this world), and you shall know that which is concealed, inasmuch as everything (both above and below) is the same. For all that the Force has created in a corporeal way has been patterned after that which is above."[8]

Thus we learn the sublime teaching that when the Kabbalah reveals the essence of unseen elements, its interpretation of the concealed will not conflict with subsequent actions and interactions. We are presented by the Zohar, therefore, with instant, immediate knowledge of the root of any matter, obviating the necessity of going through the customary procedures of trial and error.

3

THE MAJOR CONCEPTS

NOT ALL THE CONCEPTS OF KABBALAH ARE SUSCEPTIBLE TO direct description. Much of the analysis of upper and lower worlds is carried out through analogy and metaphor. Through the use of colorful images, an imaginative link is established between the phenomena being described and the tangible world in which we live; otherwise the world described by Kabbalah would remain forever closed and inaccessible. The imagery enables us to discern the reality and helps us understand more surely the consequences that flow from the inner meaning of the image.

It is for this reason that the analysis of the concept of *Yesh Me'Ayin* is central to the understanding of the purpose of this imagery.

YESH ME'AYIN, SOMETHING FROM NOTHING

> *Relationship of the metaphysical realm to the manifest universe — the metaphor of light and vessel to describe the process of spiritual levels from higher to lower — the inclusion in Creation of the facility within man to uncover the source and purpose of his creation*

We start with a world, spiritual in content, which lies beyond the immediate grasp of the senses. It is a world that exists both within and beyond our physical existence, with its own structure, modes of behavior, patterns of identity and communications; it sees without being seen. This metaphysical realm bears the same relation to the sensible world as the Creator does to the Creation, or the soul to the body. The implication of this analogy is that, in order for the transcendent to be known, it must assume the guise of the material. This has obvious echoes of the concept of *Yesh Me'Ayin*, but, whereas *Yesh Me'Ayin* is a general description of the process of the Creation, Kabbalah in its wider applications also deals with the realities of our physical existence, whether as individuals or as a people.

The most common metaphor used for describing this process from higher to lower spiritual levels involves the image of Light as the content, and the vessel as the container. These exist on all levels, whether we are dealing with different types of spiritual worlds (*olamot*), their constituent parts (*sfirot*), or with the major process by which one level is transformed into the next. The configuration of light and vessel at any particular stage in their development is called *partsuf* (face or countenance). At the very beginning of this process, is a cosmic event known as "the breaking of the vessels" (*Shvirat haKelim*) where the initial vessels through which the creation is to be formed and shaped are unable to contain the power of the spiritual light which pours into them, and shatter. Here we have a warning to future generations not to run before they can walk in spiritual matters.

The result of this cosmic explosion necessitates the formation of far more sturdy vessels which will be able to contain the light. By virtue of their thickness, however, vessels tend to hide the light they contain, and for which they are meant to act as conduits. In the final stage, where the vessels are coterminous with the tangible world of the senses, the light is practically invisible.

The very dynamism by which this process operates contains within itself its own purpose. The creator veils His *Or Ein Sof* (Eternal Light) in order to allow this world to exist in its present form. This should not be understood to mean that Creation is separated from the Creator but rather that the spiritual end-product of Creation — man — has the facility within himself to uncover the source and purpose of his own creation. This is to be achieved specifically through the tools of study, prayer and *Mitzvot*, the end goal of which is called *Dvekut*, the attachment of man to his Creator, the reunification of all vessels and lights.

Let us now examine these concepts in greater detail.

GIVING AND TAKING —
THE PURPOSE OF OUR EXISTENCE

> *The need to have a Desire to Receive to*
> *effect the goodness of the Creator — the*

requirement for a stimulus from below — the provision by the Creator as a means of performing service to eliminate Bread of Shame upon receiving the Light

The purpose of Creation, as we have said, was to impart boundless goodness to all. To complete the purpose of imparting goodness the existence of an inherent Desire to Receive is required. This Desire to Receive constitutes the vessel, indicating the exact measure of the bounty to be received, since the dimensions of the Light (forces of goodness) are in exact proportion to the Desire to Receive. The Creator in His wisdom imparts to a spiritual, metaphysical entity no more and no less than is desired; if He were to impart more Light than the vessel desired or required, this would in essence contradict the very nature of His infinite love and abundance, for there can be no degree of spiritual coercion in His goodness. To impart or share with others, on any level, can be considered noble and kind only when the recipient desires and enjoys that which is offered to him. However, when the recipient rejects the gift yet the donor continues to insist on its acceptance, one can hardly consider this an act of giving. There can be little true satisfaction to either party in a gift that is neither sought nor desired, and which is consequently misused or discarded.

It follows from this that despite His omnipotence, the Creator's beneficence cannot manifest itself or prevail without an active Desire to Receive on the part of man. This sublime idea is emphasized with striking clarity by Rabbi Shimon: "no influence from above can prevail unless it is preceded by a stimulus from below."[9] The symmetry and harmony between these opposing forces, whether we talk of them as positive and negative or cause and effect, is necessary for the continuous and uninterrupted flow of energy.

Ultimately, this law is linked with the fundamental purpose behind the giving of the Torah, with its precepts and commandments. The Zohar states:

> Since the Creator has the attribute of all-goodness, He therefore created this mundane world with its human inhabitants. Thus the Creator could now bestow upon them His infinite love and abundance.

The Zohar continues:

> However, should all this be true, if the Creator indeed desired to bestow His abundance upon humanity, then why did He cast the noble and divine souls to this earthly, sublunar plane, into bodies built of clay, where they endure sorrow, temptation and the constant trials of the demonic forces of hatred and ruthlessness which the material body imposes on the soul? He might, preferably, have maintained them in His Heavenly sphere where all spirits rejoice in Paradise, where they merit the ineffable goodness of the Divine splendor which is bestowed upon them.

The reason, according to the Zohar, is that the world was created for man with all its blessings and problems. The Creator created this world peopling it with earthly bodies through which the soul must labor and struggle. By prayer and study of Torah we can attain His objective of purification and sanctity; without the struggle this necessitates, we would be nothing more than an idle recipient of the Creator's blessing. Declares the Zohar:

> The natural consequence of eating unearned bread, of receiving something that is not earned by labor and endeavor, is embarrassment and shame! he eats the Bread of Shame.[10]

Rabbi Shimon teaches us that in order to permit us to eliminate this feeling, the Creator provided us with the means of performing service to Him so that He might bestow His ineffable Heavenly Light upon purified souls while they are still on this earthly abode. Man thus eliminates all feeling of shame. Upon receiving the Light, the soul experiences the all-goodness and perfection of its Creator and recognizes the delight and contentment which follow the successful implementation of exacting labor.

In fulfilling the precepts of the Creator with love and understanding,one is exerting one's Desire to Impart, thereby removing the bread of shame that otherwise would prevent the boundless and eternal Light from entering the soul.

GENERAL OVERVIEW OF THE DOCTRINE OF *TZIMTZUM* (RESTRICTION)

> *The yearning of the Desire to Receive to Impart — the restriction of the Divine Light to satisfy the yearning — the creation of a vacuum — the birth of primordial space and the physical universe governed by the laws of Restriction — the descent of the soul and the loss of memory of the purpose of the descent — maintaining a balance between receiving and sharing to achieve fulfillment of a permanent nature*

Tzimtzum is the process of contraction, or restriction, of the Divine Light. The Divine Light, or the Light of the Endless, is the spiritual substance that emanates from the Creator. Its essential characteristics is that it contains the potential of completely satisfying any Desire to Receive by providing its necessary fulfillment. The beneficence flows incessantly and comprises all the varied forms of spiritual nourishment displaying an infinite degree of Heavenly bliss, as we read in the words of the Prophet Isaiah "The whole world is filled with His glory".[11]

According to the Lurianic system the doctrine of *Tzimtzum*, or restriction, first occurred during the process of creation when it was executed as a voluntary restraint by the Desire to Receive because "there had arisen in His pure will the intention to create the worlds".[12] This means that within the Kingdom of *Ein Sof* which is characterized by the Desire to Receive, there was an aspiration towards achieving equality with the *Infinite Light* of the *Ein Sof* the characteristic of which is the Desire to Impart. This was made possible and was destined to be revealed through the creation and existence of our universe.

The yearning to be identified with the aspect of sharing, or imparting, which corresponds to the essence of the Infinite, grew out of the aspect of Bread of Shame resulting from the continuous receiving of the Endless Light in the Kingdom of the *Ein Sof*. The result of these two stages was the rejection, or restriction, of the Light, which created a vacuum. This vacuum, in turn, permitted the emanation and creation of all the worlds through the process of revelation.

This vacuum of limitation, which is indicative of the unfulfilled Desire to Receive, gave birth to primordial space and to the limitations of time, space and motion. Prior to the *Tzimtzum* (restriction), there had been no destructive influences at work in the universe, since there had been no desires left unfulfilled. However, due to the aspect of Bread of Shame brought about by the inability of the souls to earn the Light or to share their blessing with one another, they caused the Restriction. This, in turn, created the physical universe, which is governed by the laws of Restriction. This area of incompleteness and deficiency brought about by the self-imposed restriction of the Light ultimately leads to the chaos and lack of harmony that is called the Evil Inclination. Just as the physical veiling or screening of the light of the sun blocks its penetration, so the whole of Creation constitutes an enormous process of restriction or rejection brought about by the original *Tzimtzum* that took place in the World of the Infinite.

RESTRICTION AND THE SOUL

> *The descent of the soul to the world to correct the imbalance of receiving and sharing —the Evil Inclination causes the soul to forget its purpose — the interaction of giving must at all times be balanced*

The involuntary restriction imposed upon man is due to the nature of the soul which is transformed on leaving its domain in the upper world so that it can live inside a body of flesh and blood. In the higher worlds, the soul experiences both the beneficence of the *Ein Sof* and the feeling of shame that is a result of the inability to impart anything to the all-inclusive Infinite. Thus the soul descends to this world in order to erase the feeling of shame and thereby achieves fulfillment. However, in passing into this world the soul forgets its purpose, due to the influence of the Evil Inclination, and becomes distracted by the earthly delights of this mundane existence.

In this connection, the story is told of a poor man who found himself unable to support his family. One day, a friend told of an island so far away that it took six months to reach, where diamonds were said to be so plentiful that he would be able to bring back enough to last him a lifetime. After consulting with his family, he decided that the difficulties of the journey and the pain of separation from those he loved would be amply compensated for by the rewards he could bring back, and so he embarked on a boat bound for the wonderful island.

When the boat eventually landed, he found that his friend's report had been true; diamonds lay in great heaps wherever he looked. Quickly he set about filling pockets, bags and boxes with the precious stones, but he was interrupted by a man who informed him that there was no need to make such haste, since the boat was not due to return to his homeland for another six months. It now became clear to the traveller that he would have to find some means of earning a living during these six months since the diamonds he had collected, being so common, were of no value in this land. He made several enquiries and discovered that wax was a rare and precious commodity here, and that a man with the patience and skill to make candles would surely flourish.

Sure enough, he was soon proficient in candle-making and earned enough for a good and comfortable life on the island, only occasionally thinking with sorrow of the family he had left behind. When the time came to leave after six months, he packed a case full of his precious candles and set off for his homeland. When he reached his native shores he was greeted rapturously by his friends and family and proudly displayed the fruits of his labor — a pile of worthless candles.

So it is with the souls who descend into this world to correct the imbalance of receiving and sharing through the conditioning agent of the Torah but who neglect this spiritual purpose and become preoccupied with the concerns of the body and of this transient world.

Most people are involved only on the physical level of existence, with its ever changing environment of effects and movement. It is easy to see how the apparently varied and complex interactions of the physical world could distract the soul from its true purpose, just as the poor man was distracted from his true purpose by the necessity of earning a living. However in order to maintain a balance between taking and sharing, the concept of restriction became an integral part of our organic mechanisms. Thus in the process of receiving without having merited or earned the benefit, all the involuntary mechanisms intimately connected with our psyche become operative.

BALANCE

> *The value of balancing receiving and shar-*
> *ing — joining with the Creator in perfect*
> *union — the problem of imbalance when*
> *Desire to Receive dominates*

For one to capture and retain permanent spiritual nourishment or emotional satisfaction, the interaction of giving must at all times be balanced, thus enabling the Light of all-inclusive beneficence perpetually to illuminate each and every corner of our being.

We see this process at work every second of our lives, in the mechanism by which we draw the breath of life into our lungs and then expel it. The drawing represents the Desire to Receive, the exhaling of air the Desire to Impart; clearly the two must be in perfect balance at all times. We also notice that we must breathe in before we can breathe out, just as we must have a Desire to Receive before we can share, and we cannot exhale a greater amount of air than we breathe in. Thus the metaphysical symbol of restriction reflects a highly developed conception of the cosmological process and drama of attraction and repulsion, a drama in which the Divine scheme of man's place and function is revealed as corresponding completely to the original *Tzimtzum.*

The phase of receptivity, which forms one part of this dualism, is on a par with the Supreme Light of the Emanator and enables the created being, man, to join with the Creator in perfect union. The totality of these metaphysical forces forms a balanced and harmonious structure which is made manifest by the enveloping of the Light by the vessel of the Desire to Receive. As long as the relationship remains a directly symmetrical one, as in the *Ein Sof,* the objective of receiving fulfillment of a permanent nature can be achieved.

The Desire to Receive which, as we have seen was originally created for the sole purpose of drawing down the endless blessings of the Creator, is all too often transformed on our physical level of existence into a Desire to Receive for the body alone, without any thought of sharing. A great Desire to Receive is not, in itself, harmful in that it contains within it the constant opportunity of an equally great Desire to Share. It is only when the Desire to Receive dominates the individual so that it is no longer subject to any restraint, that imbalance occurs and the individual, by his selfish acts and thoughts, cuts himself off from the Creator and from the source of spiritual nourishment. What we find under such circumstances is an increasingly desperate pursuit of pleasure and satisfaction without the lasting aspect of the union of upper and lower worlds which comes from an awareness of the circular concept of receiving and sharing; only the vessels of pleasure are left, without the pure and everlasting joy of the Light. This is the meaning of the sages when they wrote, "He who desires money will not be satisfied with money." In all our feverish pursuit of the good things in this life, we are apt to forget that these are merely the outward forms, or vessels, of pleasure! Even if we have earned them by the standards of this world, the pleasure they contain is small and transient when compared to the enduring beneficence of the Creator that is constantly accessible to us through the Torah and its precepts, which act as a restraint and a channel of our Desire to Receive.

THE PRACTICAL APPLICATION
OF RESTRICTION

> *The purpose of restricting the Light — the benefit of the returning Light — the application of restriction to material benefits*

The concept of restriction needs to be understood, as it is applicable in our daily experience. To receive the benefits of the Light one needs to restrict it, at which point an unexpected result occurs. Instead of having lost the Light because of its restriction you have made a place for it to be received consciously and with purpose — the purpose of sharing. The direct light is too strong to be handled and would cause damage. Having done the restriction the returning Light will fulfill with comfort the Desire to Receive. In the physical world the Light may come in the form of material value or success. Here too the process of restriction applies to prepare a place for its receipt and to make certain to balance the receiving and giving.

MANKIND

> *Man as the culmination of Creation —*
> *potential energy of the earth blossoms with*
> *man's creation — the voice of the turtledove*
> *— man's thoughts and actions affecting*
> *cosmic events and man's fate — the place of*
> *religion as a spiritual experience — the link*
> *between the soul and the energy-intelligence*
> *of the blood — the soul's unquenchable*
> *yearning to be reunited with the Infinite*

The *Zohar* declares that man was created on the sixth day of the Lord's creative process. Why was the creation of man saved for last? Because he is the culmination of all that preceded. Man, within himself, is an excellent draft and skeleton of the entire cosmos. In addition to being participators, more importantly, according to the *Zohar*, humanity was given the opportunity of becoming determiners of universal and galactic activity. Man's awareness of his inter-penetration of the universe is discussed at great length in the *Zohar*.

> Rabbi Hiya commenced to discourse on the verse: "The flowers appear on earth, the time of song has come, and the voice of the turtledove is heard in our land." (Song of Songs, 2:12). He said "when the Lord created the world, He endowed the earth with all the potential energy it required but it did not spring forth until man appeared. When, however,

man was created, all the products that were latent in the earth surfaced above ground. Likewise, the heaven did not impart strength to the earth until man appeared. As it is written that all the plants were not yet on earth, the herbs of the field had not yet sprung up, the Lord had not caused it to rain upon the earth, "for there was no man to till the ground."[13]

All the products of the earth were still hidden in its inner recesses and had not yet shown themselves, the heavens refrained from pouring rain upon the earth because man had not yet been created. When, however, man appeared, the flowers grew and all of the earth's latent powers were revealed, or, in other words, "the time of song had come."

The earth was then ripe to offer up praises to the Lord, which it could not do before man was created. The voice of the turtledove refers to the power, the energy-intelligence, of the Lord, which was not active in the world until man was created. When man appeared everything appeared, and then, when man sinned, the earth was cursed and all good things departed. As it is written, "Cursed is the earth for thy sake".[14] This is reiterated in the verse, "When thou tillest the ground it shall not give its strength to you".[15] And the same condemnation is echoed in the verse, "thorns and thistles it shall bring forth to you".[16]

The relationship between the actions of man and cosmic events was again demonstrated when Noah sinned through drunkenness and the rest of the world also sinned before the Lord and the strength of the earth deserted it. This scourge continued until the patriarch, Abraham, appeared on the cosmic scene

and once again, "the blossoms appeared on the earth"
and all the powers of earth were restored. [17]

The *Zohar* maintains that man's internal activities can
determine external events. Man's thoughts influence, and are
inseparable from, the external world. A similar view is expressed in the "participant observation" theory of quantum
mechanics which also negates the idea of a clear-cut division
between events, physical objects, and human consciousness,
maintaining that the observer cannot possibly separate himself
from that which he is observing.

The Zohar abounds with references to the dominant role
played by mankind in achieving a mastery of his destiny and
the improvement of his quality of life. It places religion in a
context of spiritual experience, rather than rigid reactionary
adherence to dogmatic doctrine for the sake of the Deity. Man,
as portrayed by the Zohar, is a spiritual entity whose fate is
determined by the nature of his thoughts and actions. Thus, a
verse like, "For dust thou art and unto dust shall you return,"[18]
seems to conflict with the theme of the Zohar which states:

> Whoever labors in the Torah upholds the world as a
> whole. For as man's body consists of members and
> parts of various ranks, all acting and reacting upon
> each other so as to form one organism, so does the
> world at large consist of a hierarchy of created
> things, which when they properly act and react upon
> each other together form literally one organic
> body.[19]

The preceding Zohar stresses the intimate connection
between man and the cosmos. Compare this perspective with
the Mishnaic declaration: "Know from where you come: from

a decadent drop; where are you going: to a place of dust, worms, and maggots"(Avoth 3:1). Man is seen by the Zohar in an infinitely more positive light. The Zohar maintains that man's corporeal body should not be treated as mere flesh and bones. Man's infinite aspect, the eternal soul, must also be taken into consideration.

The Ari, Isaac Luria, stated the Kabbalistic view on this subject: "The blood of man provides the link between the soul of the upper realm and the corporeal body in the terrestrial realm". The flesh embodies the energy-intelligence of the desire to receive for oneself alone; the skin, which extends everywhere and covers everything, is a living symbol of the upper firmament; and the veins and arteries act as chariots to link the soul with the body. Blood contains both the energy-intelligence of sharing as well as the energy-intelligence that is found in all other parts of the body, the desire to receive for oneself alone.

The discovery that blood consists of red and white cells came as no surprise to the Kabbalist. Red had long been designated by Kabbalah as a color epitomizing the desire to receive, while white has been defined as a symbol of the desire to share. The blood, being the binding link between the soul and body, must, it was reasoned, contain within its molecular structure both aspects of desire. Blood unites all members of the corporeal family. When any member of the body suffers a contusion, the blood demonstrates its desire to impart by rushing to the scene of the accident. The red cells embrace the energy-intelligence of receiving, the white cells, the function of which is to destroy infection, demonstrate the opposite energy-intelligence of sharing — small wonder, then, that mankind displays schizophrenic tendencies.

The idea of the soul's unquenchable yearning to be reunited with the Infinite is a fiber woven throughout all sections of the Zohar. One of the key elements of the Zoharic world view, one could almost say the essence of it, is the concept of the unity and mutual interconnectedness of all aspects and events, in order to achieve a state of consciousness in which everything is recognized as inseparable from the single all-pervading cosmic unity. To consciously perceive and embrace the union of all of the universe's myriad manifestations is to experience the highest reality.

Explorations into the subatomic world in the twentieth century have helped to reveal the dynamic interplay within the cosmic unity. The components of an atom do not exist as isolated energy-intelligences, but rather as integral parts of an all-encompassing whole. Einstein's theories of General and Special Relativity, presaged by the author of the Zohar, also force us to abandon the rigid classical concepts of absolute time and space. From the Kabbalistic perspective, the fundamental importance of these new scientific findings is that they provide a framework for achieving altered states of consciousness through which all separate manifestations are experienced as non-delineated components in a vast intimate and integrated continuum. The Zohar, meanwhile, furnishes the mental and emotional apparatus by which an elevated awareness of the interconnectedness of past, present and future, space, time and motion, can be attained.

THE *SFIROT*

The unified energy of the Ein Sof — the ten Sfirot structured on three columns — the aspect of Light and the aspect of vessel as

> *representative of all existence — transforma-*
> *tion, the process of evolution — the polar*
> *relationship and intrinsic unity of opposites*
> *— Rabbi Ashlag's interpretation of "He and*
> *His Name are One"*

The *sfirot*, or vessels, are the system used in Kabbalah to describe the process by which the unified energy of the *Ein Sof* is diversified in its transmission from the upper world to the lower levels. Each *sfirah* represents a different form of what we might call "bottled-up energy", with characteristics and attributes. Every complete structure that manifests in the universe contains the ten *sfirot*.

These ten *sfirot* are depicted in a system of columns, referred to as the Tree of Life (see illustration in the Appendix). The *sfirot* in the right column has the characteristic of imparting, or sharing, and are positive; the *sfirot* in the left column have the characteristic of receiving, and are negative; the *sfirot* in the central column have the characteristic of balance, i.e. keeping the energy of the right and left columns in balance. Each *sfirah* (vessel) has all of the characteristics, but one is dominant.

A vessel has a definite and defining effect on the energy it receives. When we examine the two aspects — light (energy) and vessel (receiver) — from a metaphysical point of view, we discover that the vessel is the embodiment of the metaphysical, non-observable Desire to Receive.

The Desire to Receive also exists in inanimate objects — such as the light bulb — but only in its inactive form. While in the light bulb this energy is precisely governed and controlled by the laws of physics, it is only when we consider Man that we find constraints of the physical universe are lifted, requiring that we take into account the active participation of the vessel and its Desire to Receive in the whole process of transformation of the energy from one state to another.

The aspect of light and the aspect of vessel represent all of existence. The potential of light depends on how the vessel manifests. The light and the vessel exist in the metaphysical realm and can manifest on a mundane, physical plane in which the aspect of light is the Desire to Impart and the aspect of the vessel is the Desire to Receive for oneself alone.

One of the essential and striking concepts relating to the structure (*partzuf*) of the Endless, or Infinite World (*Ein Sof*) is the central role played by transformation in the process of evolution and development. All transformation is a process of cause and effect, and cause and effect are also manifest in the interplay of male energy which imparts and female energy which receives.

Ein Sof is the source from which all subsequent and lower worlds and levels of existence emanate. It operates through an interplay of opposites. There is a polar relationship of opposites throughout all levels of creation that stem from *Ein Sof* in the same way that the branch of a tree springs from and is in harmony with the hidden root. This, at first sight, would seem to be a paradox because when we are faced with opposites we usually focus on their differences instead of their affinity. The idea of an intrinsic unity of opposites seems foreign to our way of thinking, yet, according to the Kabbalistic interpretation of the original Creation, cause and effect and male and female are both polarities belonging to the realm of light and vessel. They are not delegated to different and exclusive categories. They are different aspects of the same unified manifestation of energy.

This may be compared with the positive and negative poles of an electric current which, while diametrically opposite in observable effect, are actually different manifestations of the same internal energy.

Another example that may help illustrate this point may be found in two differently colored glass containers filled with water. The water in each container appears to be a different color, but in fact, the water, representing a form of energy, is identical in both containers. Light (energy) and vessel (receiver) appear to be opposites — an extended aspect of the light energy. But in the final analysis they reduce to the same energy in that both emanate from the *Ein Sof*.

The revelation of the unity within the *Ein Sof* shook the foundation of Kabbalistic thinking. It constitutes one of the most startling and puzzling aspects of the *Ein Sof* — the idea of *"Hu uShmo Ehad"* (He and His Name are One) as interpreted by Rabbi Yehudah Ashlag. This became the root of the Kabbalistic view of the universe. "He" represents light or energy and "His Name" represents the vessel or receiver. Although diametrically opposed in terms of their essential attributes, they are recognized as two manifestations of a basic whole. This point is alluded to when evaluating the numerical values of the Hebrew words *Shmo* (His Name) and *Ratzon* (desire or vessel). They are both equal to 346. This does not mean that light and vessel are equal in terms of their respective functions, but simply that one must complement the other to produce an interplay and flow of energy. Light and vessel, while maintaining their unique individual qualities, must exist relative to one another in an all embracing unity of creation.

THE NATURE OF EACH *SFIRAH*

> *The Patriarchs as Chariots for the Sfirot —
> the first three Sfirot, part of the Sitrei Torah,
> do not affect the physical world — the na-
> ture of each of the remaining Sfirot — Zeir
> Anpin, six Sfirot*

The concept of the *sfirot* has many and wide-ranging implications in the teachings of Kabbalah. The purpose of this section is to introduce the reader in a general way to the system of *sfirot*, so that he will become aware of their occurrence and significance in subsequent studies.

The simplest way to begin to understand the *sfirot* is through the Patriarchs. Each represents a certain form of energy which is characteristic of one of the *sfirot*, and is the Chariot, or vehicle, by means of which that particular energy is brought down from its potential form in the metaphysical realm into an active form in our universe. Thus by studying the stories told in the Torah about the patriarchs, we can obtain a closer understanding of the sort of energy indicated by each of the *sfirot*.

The first three *sfirot* are the means by which Light was brought into this world; they are called *Keter* (Crown), *Hokh-mah* (Wisdom), and *Binah* (Intelligence). They are considered a part of *Sitrei Torah* and do not affect our physical world other than conducting the Light into it. Thus the first *sfirah* that we shall consider is *Hesed* (Mercy), except to note in passing that *Keter* is the purest vessel, and *Binah* is alluded to by the Kabbalist when speaking of the Force.

HESED

The energy of *Hesed* is of the right column, which represents the desire to impart. It is the energy we associate with goodness and kind actions. The patriarch who brought down this energy was Avraham who, we are told, was always ready to welcome guests into his house; this is why the Talmud says that his home had four doors — it was never closed to anyone in need. When Avraham was circumcised and in great pain, we are told that the Force caused a period of unusually hot weather, so that people would stay at home instead of disturbing Avraham's rest and recovery.[20]

GVURAH

The second of the seven *sfirot* that govern our world is called *Gvurah* (judgment), and is symbolized by the Chariot of Isaac, the son for whom Avraham waited one hundred years. The energy of *Gvurah* is called left column, because it is associated with the desire to receive. On *Rosh haShana* (New Year) we read the portion of the Law called *Akedat Yitzhak*, the binding of Isaac, which relates how the left column (Isaac) was tempered or bound by the right column (Avraham), preparing the way for the emergence of the Chariot of Jacob. Jacob represents the central column, the essential balancing factor that enables the right column to use the energy of the left without destroying it entirely. *Gvurah* represents judgment, not in the sense of punishment as we usually understand it but in the sense of the inevitable repercussions of the exercise of the desire to receive without first removing the aspect of Bread of Shame. Thus we read that "Isaac loved Esau because he did eat of his venison".[21] Esau represents the desire to receive for the body alone, without any desire to impart. Isaac is the means by which that selfish desire was transformed into a desire to receive for the sake of imparting by means of the binding of its harmful elements.

TIFERET

Jacob, as we have mentioned, represents the central column which is the *sfirah* of *Tiferet* (beauty), as is indicated by the verse, "And Esau was a cunning hunter, a man of the fields, but Jacob was a quiet man, dwelling in tents."[22] The word for "quiet" in the Torah also has the meaning of "complete" indicating that with Jacob the system of left, right and central columns was completed. The existence of the central column is the aspect that sets the children of Israel apart from all other races and peoples. It is therefore fitting that Jacob, who is also called Israel,[23] should be the father of the twelve tribes of Israel. These twelve sons, in turn, represent the twelve signs of the Zodiac which influence our world; a further example of the completeness that we associate with Jacob. It is also interesting to note, although outside the scope of this book, that the twelve tribes and the twelve signs of the Zodiac are in turn divided into four groups of three, each group being associated with either the left, right or central column.

NETZAH

The fourth Chariot is Moses, who represents the *sfirah* of *Netzah* (victory), the energy of the right column. The deeper significance of this association will be investigated in a forthcoming book on the significance and meaning of the Festivals, with particular reference to *Pesah* (Passover). For the present it is sufficient to recall the battle between the Jews and

Amalek, on which occasion Moses stood on a hill and controlled the swing of victory by raising or lowering his hands.[24]

The relationship between Moses and Rabbi Akiva, and between Moses and Rabbi Shimon bar Yohai explains why Moses was given the honor of receiving the holy Torah and why Rabbi Shimon was chosen to be the transmitter of the Zohar.

Our sages of blessed memory relate the following;[25] "The entire treasure was seen with his eye. This refers to Rabbi Akiva, for that which was not revealed to Moses was revealed to him." Nonetheless, the Talmud states[26] that Moses, through strenuous effort, eventually achieved total comprehension and understanding. A further affinity between Moses and Rabbi Akiva is indicated by our sages as follows: "There were three men who lived 120 years; Moses, Rabbi Yohanan ben Zakai and Rabbi Akiva."[27] Moses spent forty years in the house of Pharaoh, forty years in Midian, and forty years as the shepherd of Israel. Rabbi Akiva's first forty years were spent as an illiterate, his next forty as a student, and his last forty as a teacher. An even more dramatic connection is Moses' plea to the Creator that the understanding of the Torah be transmitted through Rabbi Akiva.[28]

Now it is clear that the soul of Rabbi Akiva, like the souls of all Jews past and present, was present at Mount Sinai when the Creator revealed the holy Torah to Moses;[29]why then was it to Moses that the honor of receiving the Word of the Creator was given and not to any of the other noble Jewish souls present?

Moses, as we stated, encompassed both the Inner and Encircling Lights. Their power, however, was not sufficient for him to withstand the immense infusion of Light that would be transmitted from Mount Sinai. To understand this requires consideration of the spiritual character of the archetypes of Judaism.

The Zohar states that while both Cain and Abel had aspects of the right column it was the weaker of the two in Cain, who was dominated by the left column, whereas Abel had subjected his left column to the rule of the right column.[30] Now the soul of Abel was reincarnated within Moses where its good aspects were made manifest.[31] This is the meaning of the verse which refers to the birth of Moses: "And there went a man of the house of Levi, and took to wife a daughter of Levi. And the woman conceived and bore a son. And when she saw that he was a *good* child, she hid him three months"[32]. Consequently, Moses was deemed fit to act as a Chariot for the supernal wisdom that the Creator imparted to Israel.

On the other hand, while it is obvious that Rabbi Akiva also acquired the necessary degree of spiritual consciousness, the Kabbalah tells us that the root of his soul stemmed from that of Cain.[33] This was to enable him during his lifetime to correct the predominance of the left column, so that his inner spiritual capacity could eventually strike a balance with his evil inclination. For this reason he spent the first forty years of his life, as we have said, as an illiterate, despising the scholars and learned sages of his day[34] and building up the power of his left column. So great was his spiritual potential, which he realized in the last forty years of his life that he had to enlarge the capacity of his evil inclination as spiritual anchor to his physical world.

Rabbi Shimon bar Yoḥai, as a reincarnation of Moses as we stated earlier, and also being possessed of both the Inner and

Encircling Lights, was chosen to be the transmitter of the Zohar as Moses transmitted the Torah. A further discussion of Rabbi Shimon bar Yoḥai as the transmitter of the Zohar will be found in Chapter 5.

HOD

The *sfirah* of *Hod* (glory) is represented by Aaron, who belonged to the tribe of Levites. The energy here is of the left column, *Hod* being the manifestation of the total energy of the left column in this world.[35] This is indicated by the splendor of Aaron's robes when he became *Cohen Gadol* (High Priest) (although it should be noted that the tribe of *Cohen* belongs to the right column).

YESOD (foundation)

Joseph, the son of Jacob, is also a Chariot of the central column, representing the *sfirah* of *Yesod* (foundation). It is through him that all the energy of the upper *sfirot* is brought down onto this physical level. He is the storekeeper who dispenses nourishment to the people, just as he was chosen by the Pharaoh to control the sorting and distribution of food in the years of plenty and famine in Egypt.[36]

MALKHUT (kingdom)

The last *sfirah* is *Malkhut* (kingdom), represented by David. *Malkhut* is the desire to receive, and is the world in which we live. Thus we see that David was a man of war and conflict, epitomizing the struggle for existence on this physical level. It was because of his warlike nature that he was considered unworthy to build the Temple. More than any other of the Patriarchs, he represented the battle of good and evil that is associated with the "kingdom" in which we live.[37]

ZEIR ANPIN

Six *sfirot*, namely, *Hesed, Gvurah, Tiferet, Netzah, Hod,* and *Yesod* form a group of cosmic energies referred to as *Zeir Anpin* (small face). *Zeir Anpin* and *Malkhut* are the channels of energy by which the universe became physically expressed.

This brief exposition of the nature of the *sfirot* and their connections with the Chariots of the Patriarchs should provide the beginner with some new insight into the stories of Torah. On studying them, one should bear in mind the characteristics of each *sfirah* and attempt to understand the events and actions in light of the aspect of "bottled-up energy" that each represents.

VESSELS AND LIGHTS
IN OUR PRESENT AGE

> *The Divine Light of the Creator transformed by a number of stages — the structure of Partzuf — the Lights of the soul — the spiritual character of our Age*

The Divine Light of the Creator was not concealed in one action but was gradually transformed in stages; these stages are the vessels appropriate to the quality and quantity of the Light that exists at each level of *Tzimtzum.*

Vessels are completely the opposite of Lights. The former represent the Desire to Receive, the negative aspect, while the latter express the Desire to Impart, the positive aspect. It is a law of the metaphysical realm that the first vessels to develop after the *Tzimtzum* were those with a greater degree of purity and a consequently lesser degree of the Desire to Receive. The opposite is true of the Lights; here we find that the first Lights to emerge are those with a lesser degree of the Desire to Impart, and a consequently smaller amount of energy.

The emanation of a complete structure is called *Partsuf*, or countenance. In it will always be found five *Sfirot* or levels of emanation, known as *Keter* (crown), *Hokhmah* (wisdom), *Binah* (intelligence), *Tiferet* (beauty), and *Malkhut* (kingdom). The *sfirah Tiferet* (*Zeir Anpin*) contains six *Sfirot*: *Hesed* (mercy), *Gvurah* (judgment), *Tiferet* (beauty), *Netzah* (victory), *Hod* (majesty) and *Yesod* (foundation).

Keter is the purest vessel, representing the least amount of the Desire to Receive; *Malkhut* represents the epitome and complete manifestation of the Desire to Receive. The various Lights of the soul are commonly referred to as the levels of consciousness, (the *Sfirot* being the containers). The levels of consciousness are called *Nefesh* (crude spirit), the lowest level, *Ruah* (spirit), *Neshamah* (soul), *Hayah* (living) and *Yehidah* (individual), this last being the highest and purest level of the lights. The lights of *Nefesh*, the lowest level, are first enclothed by the highest vessels, since they are also the first to issue forth from the world of *Ein Sof*. It should be clear that the upper lights, which appear later, cannot descend to their proper vessels until the lower vessels have unfolded and evolved to permit the lower lights to become enclothed by their respective vessels. This means that until *Nefesh*, the lowest level of spiritual existence, has reached the level of *Malkhut* where it is made manifest in the physical world, none of the higher lights can attain their proper vessels. The paradox we find in this process, whereby the lofty and elevated must wait for the lowly, is a profound expression of the essential duality of the universe; it also answers the question relating to the nature of the levels of spirituality that have existed through the ages, culminating in our age, which is called the Age of Messiah.

Our generation represents the lowest and final vessel of the *Partzuf*. Yet it is by virtue of the appearance of this lowly vessel that the lights of *Nefesh* can finally achieve their appointed place. In doing so, a vacuum is created in the upper vessels allowing the upper lights to be drawn down. This is the character of our age, where the gross manifestations of *Nefesh*, the lowest level of spirituality, are revealed in the existence of so many material-oriented, pleasure-seeking, non-spiritual people, while at the same time we witness the re-awakening of spirituality among the young, and advances in the world of science that threaten to destroy — literally as well as intellectually — all our established concepts of order and purpose.

The question why the full meaning of the Zohar was not revealed to earlier generations, who were without doubt on a higher level of consciousness and spirituality, and therefore more suited and prepared for it, is no longer a problem. We know that the esoteric mysteries of the Torah and the underlying reasons for the *Mitzvot* are derived from the Lights which are contained in the *Sfirot*, while the practical aspects of ceremony and ritual grow from the vessels of the *Sfirot* themselves. It follows that earlier generations, whose nature is that of lower levels of soul clothed in higher levels of vessels, were more complete and developed in the fulfillment of the observances of the practical elements of Torah, whereas our generation will bear witness to the perfect understanding that results from the complete union of the lights with their appointed vessels.

THE MIDDLE POINT

> *Nothingness, the Primordial Point, the source of all Being — description of existence within the Ein Sof — restriction as the cause of Creation — the Light and its abundance restricted itself within the middle point — the paradox of the supreme Light, with the caracteristic of only imparting, complete unity — the relationship of the Creator with His Creation and the part played by man — description and analysis of the Creator*

While many of the main teachings of Kabbalah can be stated simply, some of the concepts of Kabbalistic techniques employ highly intricate explanations and cannot be reduced to simple terms without losing their significance. One such teaching is the concept of the Middle Point, linking in many ways ideas introduced in previous discussions relating to the Creator, Creation, and Man. More specifically, the concept of the Middle Point sheds light on the difficult concept of Nothingness, both in the spiritual and physical realms. It is particularly relevant to the contemporary issues being raised in the field of physics.

The unfolding, emanation and evolution of "something from nothing" is frequently described by both the Zohar and the Ari. The symbol used to describe the chain of existence from the "hidden Cause" is the Middle or Primordial Point. This point is what Rabbi Shimon bar Yoḥai and later Kabbalists refer to as the Beginning; it is the source of all being which led to all subsequent creations. The first word of the Torah (*Bereshit* usually translated as "in the beginning") bears witness to the supreme and paramount importance of the Point of Creation. The abstruse and complex Zoharic interpretation of Creation, in which it describes the emanation of the Middle Point after restriction (*Tzimtzum*) gives a clear indication of the difficulties that will be encountered. It shows here that the entire Torah must be understood on a mystical level if it is to be understood at all. The body of the Torah is no more than a *corpus symbolicum* through which the vast fountain of the Divinity and its metaphysical concepts become revealed. Declares the Ari:

> Know that before the emanations were emanated and the creations were created, the supernal simple Light filled the entire existence (within the *Ein Sof*), and there was no empty space or vacuum whatsoever. For everything was filled with the Light of the *Ein Sof*, the Endless World. However, when the simple desire arose (and restricted itself) to permit the creation of the worlds and to emanate emanations and thus bring to fruition the perfection of its deeds, names and appellations, this (restriction) was the cause of the creation of the worlds. And behold the Light and its abundance then restricted itself within the middle point.[38]

The Middle Point is so called because it is the vessel for receiving the Endless Light, and is also known as *Sfirah* of *Malkhut*. However, before restriction the Middle Point (*Malkhut* or Kingdom) was completely and endlessly filled with the upper, supernal Light, beyond any measure or limit. Consequently, this world is designated as the *Olam Ein Sof*, the Endless world. Here where the Middle Point is united with the Light, encompassed and encircled by it, it is as if the Middle

Point were receiving the Light in the exterior of the vessel and is thus filled infinitely and perpetually. In this manner, it is possible for the Middle Point to hold immeasurable and limitless Supreme Light.

From our discussion of the Thought of Creation, we acquainted ourselves with the purpose of the Desire to Receive, which is contained within the endless Light and the Endless World. While this Desire is called the Kingdom (*Malkhut)* of the Endless, nevertheless it did not exert any limitation or circumscribe any restraint in relation to the Endless Light. At this stage of Creation, the gradations, variations and differentiations of the Desire to Receive were, as yet, unrevealed. Within the Endless World, the Desire to Receive was itself a pure Light and not separated from the Light by any discrimination or severance.

Within this absolute and indivisible unity of the Endless World, there lies a paradox. The supreme Light has the inherent characteristic only of imparting, lacking any degree of the Desire to Receive — yet this Light co-exists with the Desire to Receive which, by its very essence, should bring about a diversity or severance of some sort. At this stage, however, they are considered indiscernible and are in complete and pure unity. The reader might refer to the concept of *Dvekut* for further insight into this concept.

The Infinite Light or Vessel of the *Ein Sof*, according to Kabbalah, belongs to the area which is totally beyond human comprehension. However, the identity of the Desire to Receive with the pure Light can reveal the necessary characteristic of that Desire within the *Ein Sof* from the standpoint of Man. It signifies that the Desire to Receive, despite its innate craving for the Ineffable Goodness, is essentially an embodiment of all other positive characteristics as well — imparting, sharing or bestowing — with an admixture of personal desire and ulterior motives. The mystical interpretation of the Desire to Receive that exists concurrently with the Light within the *Ein Sof*, is known as the doctrine of the *Sfirot*. This fundamental contemplation of the union between Light and vessel is the common denominator of sharing. The desire of the Light to Impart and the transmutation of the Desire to Receive provide us with an indication of the connection between these two opposing forces in the infinite spheres which cause them to be considered inseparable and indiscernible. In this way, we can understand the sublime teaching that the Desire to Receive did not bring about any boundary or limitation upon the Endless Light, inasmuch as no diversity of essence between them had been revealed at that point.

We are more concerned, however, with the second phase of Creation, leading to an understanding of the relationship of the Creator with His Spiritual Substance of Light which He created, and with Creation itself, as well as the critical part played by man, all of which will lead to a realization of our true objectives in this world.

> Following restriction, whereby the light withdrew
> around the middle point there remained an empty
> space, atmosphere or vacuum surrounding the exact
> middle point.[39]

This vacuum after restriction should be understood as the first effect. Here lies the entire secret of Kabbalistic thought and I urge the reader to ponder this concept carefully. There is no disappearance in light or energy. This we may more fully understand through an example. A fertile male can procreate life almost all of the time. Whether this procreation actually occurs is decided by the vessel or female. If she is sterile then when the seed reaches the vessel (the womb) there is no reaction on the part of the egg. This lack of procreativity we call vacuum. The energy of the male is not diminished. It is the inability of the female to encompass and thus reveal the light or energy.

A further example of the mysteries and paradoxes which permeate the teachings of Kabbalah is the concept of "speed of light". It is a firm principle in Kabbalistic thought that light is motionless. Therefore the speed of movement can only relate to the vessel — how the vehicle revealing the energy (light bulb, or lightning) can be measured. The internal energy is immeasurable and timeless. It can be seen as a symbol of profound and penetrating vision which leads to the complete comprehension of the inner meanings and paths of Kabbalah.

Kabbalistic scholars have resorted to figurative terminology in their study of the profound mysteries of Kabbalah, using as references the material objects, ideas and functions of our ordinary world. The nature and manner of this symbolic form has been chiefly responsible for the difficulty encountered in penetrating into the depths of the inner wisdom of the Kab- balah. Nevertheless, this intricate and at times confusing maze of symbolism is the very key to its understanding. This paradox can be understood if we consider the use of imagery in other forms of writing and common usage, where we often use one concept to illuminate another. Thus, when we refer to prayers and *mitzvot* as "cables", we are using the image to emphasize the drawing aspect, or their function as paths through which certain sorts of energy can be channelled, just as electricity can be transmitted through a cable. we are not, however, referring to the physical characteristics of a cable, such as its dimen- sions, shape or color, and anyone who does not realize this is likely to mistake our original intention. It is the same with the use of images and symbols in the Kabbalah, where one specific attribute of a physical entity may be referred to by using the image of the whole entity. If we are aware of the precise usage we can learn from the symbol, but if we select the wrong attribute, or impute superfluous attributes, we will be misled. It should be borne in mind at all times that all the words of the Kabbalah are but images and symbols, since words alone cannot express the inexpressible mystery of the Creation.

In determining and expressing ideas concerned with the invisible world, the scholars of the Kabbalah have made use of the names of the tangible dimensions of this world. In effect each name symbolizes, explains, and represents its own upper entity, which is located in the constellation of the celestial regions. From this we learn that the lower realm is patterned after the upper realm, as we read in the Zohar: "Nor does the smallest blade of grass on the earth fail to have its specially appointed star in the heavens."[40]

All that exists in the celestial or supernal world will, in time prevail and show itself in a reflected image on earth, yet the totality of upper and lower worlds are always one whole entity. This provides the insight and knowledge required for our under-standing of metaphysical concepts.

When we come to consider the picture of Creation, the upper and lower worlds may be compared to a tree by which the natural laws and principles of both metaphysical and physical realms operate in our universe. It is the tree of energy, with its feedback of activity, the "Tree of Life" referred to in the Zohar[41] and the *"Etz Haim"* of the Ari, in which he devised what has come to be recognized as the most compre-hensive and lucid interpretation and systematic description of the Zohar. The Tree of Life has its roots buried deep, beyond the realm of perception; all we see are the results, or effects of that root, in the form of trunk, branches, and leaves. Thus through the principles of corresponding natures we can observe the unknown area of the upper realm by examining the interactions of that which is below. With the knowledge of Kabbalah, we can trace the origin and development of those cosmic forces and principles which ultimately influence the behavioral patterns of Man, and shape the course of mundane history.

The source of all reality takes place in the upper, undetected sphere, (the root) descending and evolving through the process of cause and effect (or imparting and receiving) in an intelligible order down to the level of our existence. The physical universe, with its cosmic elements, is the bodying forth, or evolution, of the spiritual region (trunk, branches, etc). There is no wisdom or science to be found whose objects and functions are so closely integrated as in the law of cause and effect, which is the infinite progression of the esoteric knowledge of the Kabbalah.

We can now better understand that stage in the evolutionary process of Creation in which, following the restriction of the Middle Point, which is the Desire to Receive, a vacuum or empty space was established.

At this point, declares the Ari, "there were no distinguishable or discernible levels or grades despite the withdrawal of the light."[42] Why then, we might be justified in asking, are we witnesses to a multi-faceted Creation? "The distinction of a multitude of manifestations," answers the Zohar, "is due solely and primarily to our way of perceiving the world, a result of the perception of the light by finite, created beings."[43] Furthermore, from what we have said regarding the relationship between upper and lower worlds, it must follow that the infinite manifestations of our terrestrial realm are a metaphorical indication of the yet more remotely hidden worlds of the celestial regions.

The innermost Being of the Divinity, and the Light as an extension of the Deity, motivated and initiated the creation of the soul and the *Sfirot* vessels which would ultimately enclothe it and would benefit from its beneficence. The motivating Thought of Creation, which was to impart beneficence to man through the Desire to Receive, influenced the emergence of the multiform degrees of the Desire to Receive. This is due to the fundamental characteristic of the Light, which could fill and nourish these vessels with an infinite quantity of abundance. In other words the Light, in its infinite Desire to Impart, required and caused the manifestation of a correspondingly infinite number of souls which would desire this beneficence. Thus this first and primary world, the world of *Ein Sof* (the Infinite) is given this symbolic name in accordance with the endless variety of degree of receiving that took place within the union of the Light with the Kingdom of the *Ein Sof*. In all this it should be remembered that the Divine Light itself remained a total unity, as noted in the passage. "I am the Lord, I do not change."[44]

We can compare this process of undiminished imparting to other varieties of power and energy — the endless waterfall, which can fill an infinite number of vessels without being affected, or an electric current that can supply power for a wide range of appliances which may differ in their subsequent manifestation of that power (light, heat, motion) without affecting the source of the energy. In all these cases, the division which is ultimately seen is a result of and dependent on the energy of the source with is enclothed by the vessels. In the source of the energy itself, however, there is no change.

Let us now return to the section of the Zohar that deals with the opening lines of the story of Creation, bearing in mind that the "beginning" referred to is the emergence of the Middle Point.

> When the desire of the King began to take effect, a hard spark (as from the striking of two stones, one "rejecting" the other and thus producing a spark, as with the Desire to Receive in its rejection of the flow of light from the Desire to Impart) engraved engravings in the Upper Supernal Light (thus causing a vacuum, just as in the hewing of a stone which at the moment of the chisel's stroke, leaves an empty space in the stone and causes a spark, which is otherwise known as the spark of friction). This hard spark sprang forth within the innermost recesses of the mystery of the *Olam Ein Sof*, the Endless, (the final phase of the Endless, which is referred to as *Malkhut* of the Endless World) as a potential and formless concept of aura, indiscernible and undetected wedged into a ring. This is the mystery of the Middle Point which, before Restriction, was unutterable and inexpressible, but at this stage, is expressible to the extent of being compared to a circle in that it has neither beginning nor end nor phases by which it can be detected, so that it is indiscernible. It is neither white nor black, neither red nor green.[45]

The Zohar, in stressing that it was "not black", seeks to avoid the misunderstanding that might arise when considering the restriction of the Light. Since it is discussing the withdrawal of the Light, it might seem that the state of "absence of Light" was the same as blackness, this being its customary definition. However, in its determination to render the exact nature of the stage which became manifested immediately outside . the Endless world, emerging as the act of restriction, the Zohar insists that this particular stage, being totally imperceptible, lacks any of the attributes of color — including the total lack of it.

After the *Tzimtzum*, or restriction, whereby the vessel of Malkhut (Desire to Receive) brought about a separation from and rejection of the Endless Light, the desire of the vessel was in no way diminished. We can see this from the story which appears in this book of the rich man and the poor man (page 147); when the poor man refuses the food (restriction), he does not thereby affect his hunger in any way — he merely states that he is unable to exercise his Desire to Receive under the circumstances, due to his feeling of Bread of Shame. Here too the desire for spiritual nourishment remains constant.

Since the inherent nature of the Light is to impart, it continues to attempt to fulfill the desires of the vessel, as it did continuously in the *Olam Ein Sof*. However, at the moment of restriction when the vessel brought about the separation, the Light withdrew. The Zohar talks of the return of the "Line of Light" from the *Ein Sof* because its return in its entire form would have led to the re-awakening of the feeling of Bread of Shame, since the vessel had not, at this stage, been able to do anything to share that which it wanted to receive.

The return of a circumscribed and limited measure of Light obviously failed to fill the vessel completely, as we have said. This paved the way for the vessel to overcome the Bread of Shame, which is the fundamental purpose for the creation of the worlds, culminating in the creation of our universe. Due to its insatiable desire for the limitless Goodness of the *Ein Sof*, which remained unfulfilled by the limited return of the line of Light, the Desire to Receive now became recognizable through its exertions to satisfy its desire. Prior to the Restriction, when all desires were instantly fulfilled, the Desire to Receive was motionless and indiscernible due to its union with the Light *(Dvekut)*. It is only after the separation, after the vacuum and the return of the line of Light, that an awareness of something lacking comes into being within the vessel. At that point, movement comes into being, indicating the emanation of the world of time, space and motion in which we exist, prior to our removal of that aspect of Bread of Shame and our subsequent re-unification with the Blessed world of the *Ein Sof*.

THE FIVE WORLDS

Five Degrees of Light

The process of creation resulted in five worlds consisting of five degrees of Light. The Kingdom of the Infinite is the origin of all the worlds. Each of the worlds extends from the preceding one and they are all connected. Each world contains the ten *Sfirot*. The following list is arranged in descending order of Light.

1. The Primordial Man (Adam Kadmon)

   This is the world of Keter (crown) which forms the prototype of Man and from which Man's soul derives its top degree of *Yehidah*. It consists of the ten outer *Sfirot* (the vessel), and a line of Light which forms the ten inner *Sfirot* (the soul). This is the source of the bounty received by the emanations of lower degrees of Light. In relation to the subsequent worlds it is infinite and thus it was necessary to emanate lower degrees to veil the Light.

2. The World of Emanation (*Hokhmah* — wisdom, *Atziluth*)

The Light is clothed in the first aspect of Light from which man receives the spiritual essence of *Hayah*. It is the origin of all the worlds and the root to the world of Creation, its branch. The root is clothed by its branch, concealing it from the next lower phase, thus the branch is inferior to the root. The root is the soul of the branch, animating it and setting it in motion. Each of the worlds contains the ten *Sfirot*. The *Sfirah* Kingdom is the will to receive. It is the vessel enabling it to receive the Light and bestow it to the next world below.

3. The World of Creation (*Binah* — intelligence, *Briah*)

From this world man receives the spiritual essence of *Neshamah*. It is the root to the World of Formation, its branch. This is the second aspect of the Light.

4. The World of Formation (*Tiferet* — Beauty, *Yetzirah*)

This is the World of *Zeir Anpin* (small face). From this World the spiritual essence of *Ruah* is issued to Man. This is the third aspect of Light and is the root to the World of Action.

5. The World of Action (*Malkhut* — Kingdom, *Asiyah*)

This is our world and is the Middle Point of the vacuum of Kingdom of the Infinite, the origin of all the worlds. From this world *Nefesh* is extended to Man. This is the fourth aspect of the Light.

THE *TIKUNE* PROCESS

The Function of Tikune — its role in marriage and fulfillment

The word *"tikune"* refers to the process of restoring the soul to its true unity, thereby creating a balance in the cosmic universe. The purpose of our being here is to fulfill ourselves.

Learning to share, rejecting greed that says "take it all", is the soul's mission in life — and in life after life after life, depending upon the soul's progress towards that goal. Kabbalistically speaking, attaining that goal is called making a *tikune* or correction of the soul.

By permitting a soul to sojourn in the physical world it is given an opportunity to correct misdeeds performed in previous lifetimes. Only the soul provides the force that can integrate body energy into the whole and convert the whole to a "desire to receive for the sake of imparting" and when that occurs the soul has fulfilled its destiny by balancing its *tikune*.

When pain, suffering and tragedy attend us, it is only because we have mandated them in this or in a previous lifetime and must now remove the defects they represent so that our soul can progress. There is no such thing as punishment in the *tikune* process. Its sole purpose is to move a soul toward purification. Thus, from a Kabbalistic standpoint, all forms of pain, suffering, illness and injury have their origin in *tikune* and are there to promote growth. If the soul becomes aware of its defects and brings itself into alignment with the forces of the universe and the cosmic truths of unity, the effect of pain and suffering can be prevented, or having started, can be modified.

Marriage is an opportunity for two imperfect individuals to help each other discharge their respective tikune debts and advance their spiritual undertaking. There are circumstances under which a soul will return to this earth plane solely for the purpose of helping someone else grow and fulfill the purpose of their incarnation. In addition, some few souls at the fall of Adam escaped the corruption of the "evil shells", which we call *klippot*, and from time to time they will appear to guide us along the perilous way of our lives.

The Zohar speaks of our yearning for fulfillment in its interpretation of verse 1:7 of the Song of Songs[46]

> This is the soul speaking to the Creator saying: "Tell me the mysteries of the supernal wisdom; How do you lead your flock in the upper world? Teach me some of the mysteries of the wisdom for I have not learned them. Teach me so that I will not be in shame when I come among the eternal souls, for until now I have not reflected on these mysteries.
>
> If you don't know the beauty of the fairest among women, if you don't understand the beauty of the soul, if you return and haven't reflected in the wisdom before you came here and don't know anything of the mysteries of the upper world you

aren't merited to enter here. Therefore return again.
Learn those things that the people consider to be
unimportant and know the secrets of the upper world.

Part two

ORIGINS
AND HISTORY
OF
KABBALAH

If a man loves a woman
who lives in a street of tanners, [1]
if she were not there he would never go into it,
but because she is there it seems to him like a
street of spice makers where all the sweet scents
of the world are to be found.
So "even when they are in the land of their enemies",
which is the street of tanners,
"I will not abhor or reject them",
because of that bride in their midst,
the beloved of my soul who abides there.

Zohar III, P.115b

[1] The process of tanning hides produces objectionable odors.

4

KABBALAH: A DEFINITION

The many definitions of Kabbalah — the literal meaning of the word Kabbalah — the concealed is revealed through the study of "Receiving", a clue to the title "Kabbalah" — the culmination of the Desire to Receive — the study of wisdom: understanding the Kabbalah

THE DEFINITIONS OF KABBALAH ARE MANY AND VARIED. Each academic writer on Kabbalah sees it as illuminating a different aspect of Jewish history, philosophy or religion. To the Orthodox Jew it might be another commentary on the Torah, albeit a rather exotic one; in less dedicated circles, Kabbalah has been seen as a form of clairvoyance, occultism or magic. To those of a mystical inclination, it appears as a key to immortality, the ultimate union of the soul with the Absolute, the Almighty. Yet all these definitions fall short of the real meaning of Kabbalah.

The literal meaning of the word Kabbalah is "Receiving". Thus, in the opening sentence of the *Ethics of the Fathers*, we read that "Moses received the Torah from Sinai,"[47] the word used for "received" being *"kibel"* the past tense of the verb *"l'kabel"*. It was clear to the sages that the Torah received by Moses was unique in that it contained the knowledge necessary not only for the Jews of that time, but for all generations. Thus, when Rabbi Shimon came to reveal the mystical part of the Torah in the *Zohar*, he related it closely to the written Torah so as to demonstrate that Torah and Kabbalah are but different aspects of the same essential whole. The Torah itself represents the outer shell while Kabbalah is the inner core, concealed from sight — a relationship similar to that which exists between the physical body and the soul. Torah reveals the word of the Lord, while Kabbalah reveals the concealed.

The very fact that the secrets of the universe are revealed through the study of "Receiving" tells us a great deal about the nature of existence. We learn that the Desire to Receive is the basic mechanism by which the world operates, the dynamic process at the base of all physical and metaphysical manifestations. The title gives us a clue to this fundamental law, which is expounded in the body of Kabbalistic literature.

The Desire to Receive affects all creation because it is the basis of all creation. It affects all four levels of creation — human, animal, vegetative and inanimate. In an inanimate object the Desire to Receive is small; a rock or stone is almost independent of the physical world for its existence — it needs nothing to ensure its continuing existence. Nonetheless, for it to exist at all it must contain some part of the Desire to

Receive. As we move up the evolutionary scale, we find an increasing physical dependence upon the external world for survival, culminating in Man, who has the greatest Desire to Receive of all Creation — not only for physical things, but also for intangible needs like peace, happiness and satisfaction. The culmination of the Desire to Receive is the Desire to Receive for others, which is equivalent to the Desire to Impart. We see this in its most sublime form in the celebration of the Sabbath, the high point of the Creation, which is the expression of the Creator's Desire to Impart, and Man's Desire to Receive. It is also at the root of the fundamental directive of the Holy Torah expressed by Rabbi Hillel in the words "Love your neighbor as yourself." Only when the Desire to Receive is transformed into the Desire to Impart to others is it completed — loving your neighbor, you are also, in the profoundest sense, loving yourself and, ultimately, your Creator.

The sublime teachings of Jewish mysticism are also called "The Wisdom of Kabbalah" and "The Wisdom of the Truth." The root meaning of the word "wisdom" as it is used here is alluded to by the sages[48] when they ask, "Who is wise?" and reply, "He who sees the consequences of actions." As soon as an action occurs the wise man perceives what will result from it.

Indeed, the mark of a wise man in any trade or profession is that he does not have to wait for the future to know what the future has in store; the knowledge that he possesses is at the root level, from which all subsequent actions can be known. Kabbalah, then, may be understood as the study of wisdom, allowing the individual to understand the true meaning of Creation, the root of existence, on both the physical and metaphysical levels. At the level of the root of Creation, it enables us to unravel the mysteries of the universe and be aware of the potential consequences of action. Mysticism is rendered in Hebrew as *Ḥokhmat haNistar*, "the wisdom of the hidden, or of the unknown." Although the Kabbalah freely offers us knowledge of the original causes of all things, we should remember that this is only a part of its wisdom. Rabbi Ashlag, by translating and providing commentaries to the classical works of Kabbalah, has stripped away much of the mystique surrounding *Ta'amei Torah*, so that it can be studied with profit by all who wish; *Sitrei Torah*, the concealed sections of Kabbalah, are still — and will always remain — hidden from those who might misunderstand or misuse the knowledge contained therein.

5

THE ORIGINS OF KABBALAH

THE SEFER YETZIRAH

THE FIRST KNOWN PRINTED WORK ON JEWISH MYSTICISM IS the *Sefer Yetzirah*, whose authorship has been attributed to the Patriarch Abraham. Containing ideas and concepts of the most sublime and elevated level, this text has not been used by Kabbalists of the past due to the difficulty of defining exactly the terms and hidden meanings it contains.

THE ZOHAR — ITS HISTORY

Ascribed to the saintly sage Rabbi Shimon bar Yoḥai — a disciple of Rabbi Akiva — Rabbi Shimon goes into hiding with his son for thirteen years — the compilation of the Zohar is accomplished during this period — the spiritual history of Moses and Rabbi

Shimon — why Rabbi Shimon was chosen to write the Zohar

The most elaborate and lengthy work to have appeared in Jewish esoteric studies is the Zohar. Those who have studied it and fully understand the significance of its teachings are unanimous in ascribing it to the saintly sage of the Mishnaic period, Rabbi Shimon bar Yohai. The authorship of the Zohar is a subject of debate among those who study Kabbalah as an academic pastime, without ever attempting to understand the content of the works they analyze. Many of these scholars maintain that the Zohar was written by the 11th century Kabbalist, Moses de Leon, of blessed memory, or by others among his contemporaries. When the holy Zohar is better understood, however, it becomes evident that only someone of the stature and spirituality of Rabbi Shimon could have composed the work.

We know that each generation of Jews has a lesser understanding of Torah than its antecedent.[49] To credit a work such as the Zohar to any age other than that of the *Tannaim*, the compilers of the *Mishnah* who lived from the first to the third centuries C.E., is simply not possible, since this would imply that the level of spiritual consciousness and understanding of Moses de Leon was comparable to, if not higher than, that of the saintly *Tannaim*. When the historians elect Moses De Leon as the author of the Zohar, they thereby neglect the opinion of such great Kabbalists as Moses Cordovero, Shlomo Alkabetz, Joseph Caro, Isaac Luria, Moses Luzzato and many others — men for whom the Zohar was a way of life, rather than a field of study, and who were unanimous in their agreement that Rabbi Shimon was the author of the Zohar. The underlying assumptions of these great men were that the man who wrote the Zohar must have been on the same level of spirituality as its contents, and that only Rabbi Shimon fit that description.

Let us now, therefore, look at the history of this great sage in an attempt to understand the verdict of the famous Kabbalists mentioned above.

When Israel was under the rule of Rome, Rabbi Shimon was a disciple of Rabbi Akiva, who continued to teach Torah despite the Roman decree forbidding its study. Rabbi Akiva was captured and put to death, whereupon Rabbi Shimon launched a verbal attack on the Romans, accusing them of intolerance and cruelty, and was himself sentenced to death as a result. He fled with his son Elazar to a cave in the mountains near the Galilean town of Pki'in, where he hid for thirteen years, until the Emperor's death made it safe for them to leave.

As to the revelation of the holy Zohar, the sages of blessed memory, relate the following legend.[50] The thirteen years that Rabbi Shimon and his son spent in the cave marked a turning point in the history of the great body of Jewish esoteric knowledge. In the seclusion of the cave Rabbi Shimon was visited twice a day by the prophet Elijah, who revealed to him the secrets of the Zohar. The deeper and more comprehensive sections, known as the *Ra'aya MeHemna*, are a record of the discourses that also took place between Rabbi Shimon and Moses himself, the beloved shepherd of the title.

One should not take this to mean that the secrets of the Zohar were revealed only to Rabbi Shimon. His teacher, Rabbi Akiva, and several others before him, were fully versed in all the teachings of the Zohar. In fact, the entire understanding of Kabbalah was presented in its oral form to Israel on Mount Sinai. Many understood the dazzling truths of Jewish mysticism, but few could make others see and understand. For this, the written text of the Zohar, Jewry would have to wait for Pki'in and Rabbi Shimon.

The question still remains, however, why Rabbi Shimon was chosen to set down the teachings of the Zohar in preference to his teacher, Rabbi Akiva, or indeed any of the other giants of the Kabbalah who preceded him. This problem has been the source of many commentaries and parables; it is often stressed, for instance, that through his fugitive and solitary life, Rabbi Shimon was able to overcome the physical restraints and limitations that normally prevent the attainment of higher levels of spiritual consciousness. He was thus able to transcend the laws governing time and space, thereby acquiring root knowledge of all existence as we experience it on this earthly plane. Thus we find in the Zohar not only discussions of strictly spiritual matters but also fundamental concepts in such fields as medicine, astrology, law, telecommunications, and psychiatry. But the problem still remains — why was Rabbi Shimon chosen to live in a cave for thirteen years? The answer is to be found in the spiritual history of Moses and Rabbi Shimon as described below and also in chapter 3 in the discussion of the *sfirah Netzah*.

Within the physical body of Man we find two distinct motivating factors called the Inner Light and the Encircling Light. The Inner Light is the element of light contained within Man upon his descent into this mundane world at birth, and accompanies the individual as an aid in the pursuit of spiritual ascent. The Encircling Light is the level of consciousness which the individual merits during his or her lifetime through good deeds and actions; it is acquired gradually and is not present at birth. The Encircling Light level of consciousness is unlimited, depending on how well the individual is able to subordinate the physical body to the Light. The degree to which an individual is limited by the constraints of time, space, and motion — the physical laws of the universe — is dependent on the degree to which he or she manages to control the body's Desire to Receive (the evil inclination). Gradually, Man acquires the Encircling Light and ascends the ladder of spirituality.

The Ari (Rabbi Isaac Luria), explaining the inner makeup of Moses, states that:

> Moses encompassed the Inner and Encircling Lights; the inclusion of the Inner Light is alluded to by the verse "and she saw he was good" (Exodus 2:2), and the Encircling Light is denoted by the verse "the skin of his face shone" (Exodus 34:30).[51]

These two qualities were required before Moses could have received the entire Torah including, as I have said, the understanding of Kabbalah and the explanations of its esoteric meanings.

We learn that Rabbi Shimon was a reincarnation of Moses himself,[52] in reference to which the Zohar says

> The son of Yoḥai (meaning Rabbi Shimon) knows how to observe his ways; if he ventures into the deep sea, he looks all round before entering, in order to establish how he will accomplish the task in one attempt.[53]

From this statement the Ari draws the following conclusions:[54]

One must understand that among the souls of the righteous, there are those who possess the Encircling Light, and who have the capability of communicating the esoteric mysteries of the Torah by means of concealment and cryptic references, so as to prevent those who lack merit from understanding it. Rabbi Shimon's soul incorporated the Encircling Light from birth; he thus had the power to enclothe the esoteric lore and also to discourse on it. Subsequently permission was granted to Rabbi Shimon to write the Book of Splendor: The sanction to write this book of wisdom was not given to the sages who preceded Rabbi Shimon because, even though they were highly knowledgeable in this wisdom, even to the extent of exceeding Rabbi Shimon, they lacked his ability to enclothe and to protect the esoteric lore. This is the meaning of the reference to Rabbi Shimon made above.

THE ZOHAR — ITS CONTENT

The highly esoteric nature of its teaching and the difficulty with its language of partly Aramaic and partly ancient Hebrew — a disclosure of the hidden meaning of the Torah comprising ten sections — the spiritual value of owning and scanning the Zohar.

If the world's literature holds any volumes which might truly be designated as being complete, or, in the language of Kabbalah, as being "sealed with ten seals," that work is the Zohar. Since its completion some two thousand years ago, few works have exercised as much influence on humankind. The Zohar is the fundamental work of the Kabbalah and, thus, the premier textbook of Jewish mysticism. However, because of the highly esoteric nature of its teaching, not to mention the difficulties presented by its original language, which was partly Aramaic and partly ancient Hebrew, the Zohar, which is an extension of the enigmatic *Book of Formation*, authored by the patriarch, Abraham, remained, for centuries, inaccessible to all but a few learned and carefully chosen initiates — a situation that might be aptly paralleled with the condition extant today relative to the "average" person's lack of knowledge concerning the secret rites of science.

The Zohar, *The Book of Splendor*, was for centuries widely revered as a sacred text of unquestionable value, and in certain communities it is still esteemed and studied to this day. When the State of Israel came into existence the Jews of Yemen, a remote and isolated principality in southern Arabia, were forced to abandon nearly all of their worldly possessions as they emigrated aboard aircrafts which they referred to as "magic carpets," but the one belonging that many of them refused to part with was their copy of the Zohar.

The Jews of Yemen, of course, represent the exception and not the rule. Today, for the most part, the mystical texts, with their intricate symbolism, are ignored and all but forgotten. Knowing nothing of its underlying paradigm — utterly alien to that of Descartes — those who pick up the Zohar today are apt to dismiss it as being nothing more than mystical poetry, of no value to the modern world. Thus, an immense body of esoteric knowledge remains sadly neglected. Once considered vital to the quest for personal understanding, the wisdom of the Zohar now lies buried so deeply beneath the heavy trappings of Newtonian science, technology, and the dubious "benefits" of Cartesian education that the vast majority of people know nothing of the ancient mystical traditions, and hence, have no idea as to their sagacity and enduring vitality.

The Zohar is in the form of a commentary on the Bible. It is a record of the discourses of Rabbi Shimon bar Yohai, who lived in the second century of the common era. The *Tikune Zohar* contains an account of how Rabbi Shimon and his son Rabbi Elazar, to escape the fury of Roman persecution, sought refuge in a cave and were forced to remain there for thirteen years. During this lengthy period of exile, the father and the son gave themselves over to discovering the reality of the universe.

The Zohar contains several sections. The main section, which bears the general title of *Sefer haZohar,* is generally connected and related to the weekly portion of the Torah. To this are attached: (1) *Idra Rabbah* (Greater Assembly), which was written when Rabbi Shimon and his son Elazar emerged from the cave and selected eight disciples, who, together with himself and his son, formed the "Great Assembly," where, for the first time, the esoteric, internal teachings of the Torah were revealed; (2) *Sifra diTzenuta* (The Book of the Veiled Mystery), inserted before *Parashat Tzaveh,* deals with the structure of the creative process; (3) *Sitrei Torah* (Secrets of the Torah) treats essentially the power of the Divine Names and how they are used to tap the immense power of the cosmos; (4) *Idra Zuta* (The Lesser Assembly) describes those teachings of Rabbi Shimon bar Yohai which were not revealed during the Greater Assembly, but on the day of Rabbi Shimon's death; (5) *Ra'aya Mehemna* (Faithful Shepherd), the faithful shepherd being Moses, deals with those cosmic precepts and doctrines not covered in the discourses between Elijah the Prophet and Rabbi Shimon bar Yohai; (6) *Midrash haNe'elam* (Recondite Exposition), contains a vast collection of Scriptural exposition concerning the method of numerology, i.e., the permutations and combinations of the letters of the Aleph Beth and the Hebrew numerals; (7) *Zohar Hadash* (The New Zohar) is an independent commentary along the same lines as the Zohar, but it embraces, in addition to the Torah, the Five Megillot (Scrolls): The Song of Songs, Ruth , Lamentations, Ecclesiastes, and Esther; (8) *Tikunei Zohar* (Emendations of the Zohar) addresses the same general subject matter as the Zohar, but also discourses upon teachings which are specifically directed to the Age of Aquarius; (9) *Tosefta* (Additions) adds some fragmentary supplements to the Zohar in which references to the *Sfirot* are made.

The Zohar is more than just a commentary on the Torah. In fact, in the Zohar's own words, a literal translation of the Bible is virtually worthless. It is most interesting to read the Zoharic words on a true veracity of Biblical exegesis, which stops just short of a complete repudiation of any literal translation or understanding of the Bible.

The Zohar declares, "Woe unto those who see in the Torah nothing but simple narratives and ordinary words." The truth of the matter is that every word of the Bible contains a sublime coded mystery which, when deciphered, reveals a wealth of elevated meaning. The narratives of the Torah are but outer garments in which the real meaning is clothed. And woe unto him who mistakes the outer garment for the Bible itself. This was precisely the idea to which King David addressed himself when he declared, "Open my eyes that I might behold wondrous things from your Torah."

Another passage from the Zohar states this same sentiment, when it queries, "If the Torah merely consisted of ordinary words and narratives like the stories of Esau, Hagar and Laban, or like the words spoken by the donkey of Balaam, or even by Balaam himself, why should the Torah have been referred to as *Torat Emet*, the Torah of Truth?"

Concealed within these statements is hidden what is perhaps the quintessence of Kabbalah. The Kabbalist simply cannot accept a diluted version of so important a document as that which came with the Revelations on Mount Sinai. He loathes the tedious, prosaic interpretations of the Scriptures that often pass for contemporary Judaism, for they create the mistaken impression that Judaism, as well as other religions established according to the principles of Mount Sinai, is nothing more than exercises in robotic legalism, completely divested of spirituality — formal, fossilized systems of "do's and don'ts" that completely deny the freedom of the individual.

The spiritual and esoteric study of the Torah and Talmud is the essence of the Kabbalah. For those seeking to improve the quality of both their mental and physical wellbeing, the Zohar provides us with an opportunity to become masters of our fate, captains of our destiny. Illustrations of the way in which the Zohar interpenetrates the external shell of Torah in order to extract the esoteric kernel, could, if space allowed, be furnished on each and every verse and letter. I will only quote some examples of Zoharic exegesis on the *Parashah* to illustrate the point that the Bible is incomprehensible without the assistance and clarification of the Zohar.

> And the Lord said unto Moses, Go in unto Pharaoh,
> for I have hardened his heart.[55]

To translate the Hebrew *Bo* (come), as it appears in the original text of the Bible, as meaning "go" is a demeaning corruption of so valuable a document. Rabbi Shimon wrote:[56]

It is now fitting to reveal mysteries connected with that which is above and that which is below. Why is it written here: "Come (*Bo*) unto Pharaoh"? Ought it not rather to have said, "go" (*Lekh*)? The Lord summoned and called Moses to "come" into the celestial realm, guiding Moses through a labyrinth right into the abode of the supernal mighty dragon (Egypt's celestial representative) from whom many lesser dragons emanate.

Another fine example of the Zohar's penetrating insight into the cosmic code of the Bible concerns the almost impregnable fortress of mystery surrounding Genesis I.

Rabbi Shimon then proceeded, taking as his text: "See now that I, I am He, and Elokim is not with Me...[57]. He said: Friends, here are some profound mysteries which I desire to reveal to you now that permission has been given to utter them. Who is it that says, "See now that I, I am He"? This is the Cause which is above all those on high. That which is called the Cause of causes. It is above those other causes, since none of those causes does anything till it obtains permission from that which is above it, as we pointed out above in respect to the expression, "Let us make man." (Genesis, ch.1:26) "Us" certainly refers to two, of which one said to the other above it, "let us make."... . [There are not two Lords. The verse only refers to the permission and direction of the one above it, since the one above did nothing without consulting its colleague]. But that which is called "the Cause above all causes", which has no superior or even equal, as it is written, "To whom shall you liken me, that I should be equal"? (Isaiah, ch.40:25), said, "See now that I, I am he, and *Elokim* is not with Me," from whom He should take counsel, like that of which it is written "And God said, Let us make man."

... They [the students or Rabbi Shimon] all rose and prostrated themselves before him saying, "happy is the man whose Master agrees with him in the exposition of hidden mysteries of the Bible which have not been revealed to the Holy Angels.[58]

The Bible has long been viewed by many as nothing more than a collection of religious morality tales. Seen from a Zoharic perspective, the Bible is not intended merely to improve the outward conduct of mankind, but to assist each individual in creating an intimate personal relationship with the universe. In ancient times, the most mundane events in everyday life and customs were associated with the grandeur of the cosmos. Even the treatment of jaundice with pigeons was identified with the deepest cosmological mysteries. Our ancestors were eager to understand the universe, but its secrets were revealed to only a select few.

This is not a book about religion. Rather, the Zohar is concerned with the relationships between the unseen forces of the cosmos and their impact on man. In essence, the Bible, upon which the Zohar is based, is a cosmic code which the Zohar deciphers and reveals. Rabbi Ashlag aimed at bringing back to the collective consciousness a breath of that mystic sentiment and feeling which is the aromatic life-essence of human satisfaction and world harmony. "Kabbalah," taught Rabbi Ashlag, "is essential and indispensable for the mental and physical well-being of earth's inhabitants. It can lead to the Messianic dream of peace on earth and goodwill towards our fellow man."

The Zohar promises that with the ushering in of the Age of Aquarius, the cosmos will become readily accessible to human understanding. Already, for the perceptive observer, there are signs — such as the recent developments in quantum physics — that this revolution is already underway. It is becoming increasingly apparent that, in a very real and profound sense, man and the cosmos are inseparable.

The book which first and foremost provided the solutions to human conflicts and gave mankind an overpowering momentum to see the light of day was the Zohar. Through the Zohar one can raise his or her consciousness and transcend the crushing weight of earthly concerns. In the right hands, it is a tool of immense power. It can, when correctly perceived, provide answers to man's most seemingly baffling problems. It was and continues to be a people's book, striking a sympathetic chord in the hearts and minds of those who long for peace, truth, and relief from suffering. In the face of crises and catastrophe, it has the ability to resolve agonizing human afflictions by restoring each individual's relationship with the Divine. The Zohar has been published in a set of 24 volumes. The placement of these volumes within the home or office infuses it with its light, spreading harmony in the atmosphere and among its inhabitants. The scanning alone of its letters and words, will have the result of comforting the body and restoring balance even when one cannot pronounce the words or know the meaning. Spiritual values have their own system of making impressions.

6

RABBI SHIMON BAR YOHAI
& THE GREATER ASSEMBLY

The formation of the Great Assembly: Rabbi Shimon, his son Elazar, and eight disciples — The study of divine secrets and mysteries — The spiritual power of Rabbi Shimon — His confrontation with an angel — His power over the Angel of Death — The day of his death, known as the lesser assembly — His burial on mount Meron, a place of pilgrimage

A CONVENIENT AND VALUABLE METHOD OF STUDYING THE historical development of Kabbalah is to examine the lives and personalities of the exceptional individuals who were chosen to disseminate its teachings. Among these men the foremost group was that of Rabbi Shimon and his followers.

It is told that when Rabbi Shimon emerged from the cave in which he and his son Elazar had spent thirteen years learning the secrets of Kabbalah, his body was covered with sores. His father-in-law, Rabbi Pinḥas, wept bitterly when he saw the state of Rabbi Shimon's body, saying, "How bitter it is for me to see you in such a state!" Whereupon Rabbi Shimon replied, "I am happy that you see me like this, otherwise I would not be what I am."[59] Clearly he regarded his physical condition and discomfort as unimportant, even necessary for him to have reached the spiritual heights that he had attained.

Rabbi Shimon went on to select eight disciples,[60] who, together with himself and his son, formed the "Great Assembly".[61] They chose a spot on the road from Meron to Safed in Galilee and began to discuss the hidden meanings and mysteries of Torah that had been revealed to their teacher. Rabbi Shimon taught his disciples both *Sitrei Torah* and *Ta'amei Torah*. He revealed the Divine secrets, going back to the period before even the primal vessels had been formed. It was necessary for him to transmit ideas even if they were sometimes unintelligible to his audience, so that they would not be lost to future generations.

Before the Assembly was disbanded, however, three of the disciples — Rabbi Yosi ben Jacob, Rabbi Ḥizkiah and Rabbi Yisa — died. They had absorbed as much spiritual light as their capacity allowed and had thus moved beyond the physical sphere. Those students who were left saw the three being called away by angels.

Rabbi Shimon wept and said, "Is it possible that we are being punished for revealing that which has been hidden since Moses stood on Mount Sinai?"[62] At that moment a voice exclaimed from above, "Praiseworthy are you, Shimon bar

Yohai, praiseworthy is your portion and the portion of your Assembly. Through you was revealed that which was not revealed even to the upper Celestial Hosts. Therefore, praiseworthy is your portion. Your three students departed because their lives were fulfilled."

The light that emanated from Rabbi Shimon was of such intensity that it was said to resemble the reality that will exist at the end of the period of correction (*Gmar haTikun*), the period in which we now live, when we enter the Age of the Messiah.[63] The vessels of the three students came from the lower spheres and consequently could not contain or endure the light that had entered them, just as ordinary glass cannot withstand boiling water.

Such was the power of the author of the Zohar, a man who had truly transcended the limitations of time, space and motion.

> One day Rabbi Shimon observed that the world was covered by darkness and that the Light was concealed. His son, Rabbi Elazar, said to him, "Let us try to find out what the Creator means to accomplish."
>
> They found an angel who appeared to them in the form of a great mountain, spewing forth thirty torches of fire, and Rabbi Shimon asked him what he intended to do. "I am instructed to destroy the world", replied the angel, "because mankind does not contain in its midst thirty righteous individuals." Rabbi Shimon said to the Angel "Go before the Creator, and tell him that Bar Yohai is among the inhabitants of the world, and his merit is equal to that of thirty righteous men."

The angel ascended to the Creator and exclaimed, "Lord of the universe, are You aware of Bar Yoḥai's words to me?" Whereupon the Creator replied, "Descend and destroy the world as you were commanded: take no notice of Bar Yoḥai!"

Seeing the angel reappear, Rabbi Shimon told him, "If you do not ascend again to the Almighty with my request, I shall prevent you from ever reaching the heavens again; and this time, when you come before the Creator repeat to Him that if the world lacks thirty righteous men, He should spare it for the sake of ten; if there are not ten such men to be found in the whole world, then ask Him to spare mankind for the sake of two men, my son and I; and if you deem these two insufficient, then preserve the world for the sake of one man and I am that one. For it is written, "But the righteous is an everlasting foundation" (Proverbs 10:25).

At that very moment a voice from Heaven was heard, saying, "Praiseworthy is your portion Shimon bar Yoḥai, for the Lord above issues a decree, and you seek to countermand it; surely for you is written the verse: He will fulfill the desire of those who fear Him!" (Psalms 145:19).[64]

Here we see Rabbi Shimon, through the power of his Inner and Encircling Light, going so far as to challenge the authority of the Creator, so firmly did he believe in the justice of his cause. But his power was not only used in this way to ward off the encroaching darkness! He struggled throughout his life to introduce Light into places where ignorance and superstition reigned, to make the metaphysical as well as the physical world comprehensible, and to link all the levels of existence to reveal a world of true beauty and harmony.

So pure and righteous was the soul of Rabbi Shimon that the Angel of Death could never utter his name. Whenever the Angel of Death appeared before the Creator demanding the death of an individual, he would cite the evil deed which necessitated the death penalty. When it came to Rabbi Shimon, however, he could find no evil deeds to hold against him.[65] Then one day the *Yetser Hara* (The Evil Inclination) appeared before the Creator and demanded that He immediately recall Rabbi Shimon from his earthly abode to his rightful place in the Garden of Eden. This was a strange request, a departure from the normal procedure. The Evil Inclination usually demands the recall of an individual for the express purpose of imposing justice, punishment, or even death. But the plea of the Evil Inclination for the recall of Rabbi Shimon went as follows:[66]

> My purpose in the physical world is to divert the individual from a humane and righteous path to one of wrongdoing. But I have never before encountered a man like Rabbi Shimon bar Yoḥai. Not only have I been unsuccessful in my attempts to divert him from the proper course of piety and righteousness, but he has actually sought me out that he might be confronted with temptation, in order to turn this temptation to some useful and fruitful purpose. You must remove him from the world. I have nowhere to conceal myself from him and I fear that my objective in this physical world will fail.

For this reason alone, Rabbi Shimon was summoned to the Garden of Eden. The day of his death, known as the Smaller or Lesser Assembly, was no ordinary day. On the day that Rabbi

Shimon desired to leave this world, he prepared his final words. To all his friends gathered beside him, he revealed new esoteric mysteries. Rabbi Abba wrote,[67]

> The Light was so great that I could not approach him. When the Light departed, I saw that the Holy Light (Rabbi Shimon) had left this world. His son, Rabbi Elazar, took his father's hands and kissed them saying, "My father, my father, there were three and only one is now left." (The reference is to Rabbi Shimon, his father-in-law Rabbi Pinhas and Rabbi Elazar.)

> The people of the surrounding communities assembled, each demanding that the Rabbi be buried in their midst; then the bed upon which the body lay rose up and flew through the air, preceded by a torch of fire, until it reached the cave at Meron. Here it descended, and everyone knew that Rabbi Shimon had reached his final resting place. All this took place on the thirty-third day of the Omer, which is the eighteenth day of the month of Iyar.

To this very day, tens of thousands of pilgrims make the journey to Meron to pay tribute to Rabbi Shimon. Others come in the hope of finding an answer to their prayers and fulfillment of their needs, through the influence of *haMaor haKadosh*, the Holy Light, Rabbi Shimon bar Yohai.

7

THE GOLDEN AGE OF SAFED

SETTING THE STAGE IN SAFED

> *The expulsion of the Jews from Spain in 1492 — the destruction of the First and Second Temples fifteen centuries earlier — migration to the Middle East with some attracted to Safed — the resurgence of the study of Kabbalah in Safed — the importance of the coincidence of the migration toward the spiritual center of Safed and fifteen centuries earlier the revelation of the Zohar by Rabbi Shimon.*

IN THE YEAR 1492 OF THE PRESENT ERA, A TRAGEDY FOR THE Jewish people occurred in Spain when Queen Isabella and King Ferdinand issued a decree of expulsion that sealed the fate of the Jews in that country. All Jews who refused to renounce their faith within a stated four-month period would be compelled to leave Spain. A great center of Jewish learning, one which had profoundly influenced Jewish thought and expression, was in ruins.

In the wake of this spiritual and physical upheaval, many Jews migrated to the Middle East. A number of them settled in the Upper Galilee, drawn to the ancient town of Safed; here a group of Jewish mystics was setting the stage for the numerous mystical movements of the next four hundred years, among them being the resurgence of interest in the study of Kabbalah. From a practical viewpoint, one may attribute the sudden popularity of Kabbalah directly to the misfortunes that overtook the Jews in Spain. Their "Golden Age" having been forcibly brought to a close and their future uncertain, they sought to understand the reasons for their suffering. The philosophical teachings of the day were not sufficient to explain away the overwhelming burdens that had been suddenly thrust upon them, and they came to view Kabbalah as a means of clarifying and solving the puzzling complexities of existence.

This great convergence on Safed of mystically oriented people was by no means a coincidence. They were re-enacting a scene that had taken place some fifteen hundred years earlier. The date of the expulsion from Spain, the ninth day of Av, was also the date of the destruction of the First and Second Temples. Shortly after the destruction of the Second Temple in 70 C.E., Rabbi Shimon had revealed the Zohar. Fifteen centuries later, following the destruction of the Sephardic community in Spain, the practical application of this esoteric wisdom would become an integral part of Jewish tradition and learning. The great spiritual personalities of the time had returned to the source, their place of origin, the Land of Israel. The historical interpretation of the events of this period serves to demonstrate the inadequacy of a methodology based on superficialities. To dismiss the rebirth of Kabbalah in Safed as nothing more than the product of the expulsion from Spain and the subsequent Messianic hope centered in the Holy Land is to ignore the real significance of what had happened. Cause and effect, serving as the raw material of the historian, are of only limited use, since they are obvious only when bound together closely by time. No historian is going to risk his reputation on the association of a sequence of two events that took place fifteen centuries apart, yet this is where the truth lies. The coming together of so many spiritual individuals was unparalleled in an age when only the Spanish Jews moved in numbers to Israel, although the oppression of Jewish communities was widespread.

It is certainly true that the idea of the Messiah was closely linked to this migration, but the expectation of the imminent arrival of the Messiah was not one of the factors. It was, rather, the realization stemming from the world of the Kabbalah, that the redemption of the Jewish people and of mankind as a whole was deeply linked with the land of Israel. In Isaiah's prophetic vision of the future, he states: "For out of Zion shall go forth the Law, and the word of the Lord from Jerusalem:"[68] There is an apparent contradiction here since the Israelites had already received the Law from Mount Sinai, which was not within the boundaries of Israel; nor did the Law go forth from Zion or Jerusalem. What, then, did the Prophet Isaiah mean by this passage?

The Zohar compares the Pentateuch, the Five Books of the Law, to the body of man, and the Kabbalah to the soul; thus the "body" of the law was given on Mount Sinai, but the inner meaning, the "soul" of the Torah in its written form, would wait to be revealed from the Land of Israel. This revelation is the instrument by which Israel and the rest of the world will finally be redeemed, realizing the dream of "peace on earth, goodwill to all men."

PREPARING THE ROAD TO REDEMPTION

The Divine plan of redemption — the study of the Kabbalah flourishes with the application of Rabbi Shimon's interpretation — the resulting preservation of the principles of the Torah.

Thus the migration to Israel can be seen as part of the Divine plan, the next step on the road to redemption. The great minds of mysticism were to gather in Safed to prepare the necessary texts that would, in time, enable the Jewish community as a whole to comprehend the soul of Torah — the Kabbalah.

In Safed the Jews of Spain and nearby Provence lived a simple, religious life, seeking only peace and piety. With Rabbi Shimon's interpretation of the true meaning of Torah as their foundation, Kabbalah flourished as never before. This influence was most strongly felt in the schools of Rabbi Moses Cordovero and Rabbi Isaac Luria, two of the most important centers of study in 16th-century Safed. As the Sephardic community spread out, the study of Kabbalah extended to Italy and Turkey. In Salonika, then part of Turkey, Solomon Alkabetz (1505-1584), the composer of the Sabbath hymn *Lekha Dodi* (Come, My Beloved), established a center for the teaching of Kabbalah;

shortly afterwards, he, too, was drawn to Safed, to take part in the great revitalization of Torah then taking place there.

The Kabbalists of Safed made a conscious effort to preserve the entire Torah, with its fundamental principles and laws, by extending it so that its relevance to all aspects of life could be seen. Evolving from the structure of traditional Rabbinic Judaism, it strove to present a religious experience that would provide its adherents with sufficient energy to meet the demands of daily life. Many of the practices of Judaism — such as the three festivals of pilgrimage,[69] the religious laws and rituals relating to an agrarian lifestyle[70], had become obsolete for the Jews of Israel and the Diaspora following the destruction of the Second Temple. The survival of Judaism as a living religious system depended on the ability of the Torah to improve the lives of Jews from many different cultural backgrounds.

RABBI MOSES CORDOVERO

A brief history of his life and his contributions of priceless teachings

Rabbi Moses Cordovero was drawn "as by a thirst" to the wisdom of Kabbalah in 1522; he studied in Safed with Rabbi Solomon Alkabetz, whose sister he married. He proved a gifted teacher and writer, composing the first comprehensive commentary on the Zohar (*Or Yakar*, the Exalted Light). The manuscript, obtained on microfilm from the Vatican Library, has already yielded many volumes of priceless teachings. His other major works include *Or Ne'erav, Shiur Komah, Tomer Deborah*, and *Pardes Rimonim*.

RABBI ISAAC LURIA

> *A history of his life — thirteen years as a
> hermit studying the Kabbalah — the contri-
> bution of the Lurianic method for under-
> standing the mysteries of the Zohar — his
> unique spiritual identity and connection with
> the spirit of Rabbi Shimon — the teaching of
> the meaning of "Messiah" — the teaching of
> the falling away of physical limitations when
> the soul dominates the body*

Rabbi Isaac Luria, the *Ari haKadosh* ("Holy Lion"), was
born in Jerusalem in 1534. According to legend the Prophet
Elijah appeared at his circumcision ceremony to act as Sandak
(godfather), and told his father to take great care of the child,
for he would be the source of an exalted light. After the death
of his father, his mother, who was of Sephardic descent, took
him to the home of her brother Mordekhai Francis, a wealthy
and respected man in the Jewish community of Cairo. In Egypt,
he studied with the famous Rabbis Betzalel and David Zimra
(the Radbaz). At the age of seventeen he married one of his
cousins.

The Ari was a Talmudic authority before he had reached the
age of twenty, and soon mastered all the material his mentors
had to offer him. He then discovered the Zohar, and lived as a
hermit in a remote place by the Nile for thirteen years while he
studied the secrets of the Kabbalah. In 1569 he settled in Safed,
where he studied with Moses Cordovero and a circle of devoted
disciples until he became a master in his own right.

The Ari developed a new system for understanding the
mysteries of the Zohar: called the Lurianic method, it focuses

on the Ten Sfirot or Luminous Emanations, and sheds new light on the hidden wisdom of the Kabbalah. His complete understanding of the mysteries of the Zohar, together with the other great powers that he manifested during his lifetime, were a result of his unique spiritual identity. His student, Haim Vital, tells the following story:[71]

> One day I went with my teacher [the Ari] to the site where Rabbi Shimon and his disciples had assembled and created the Greater Assembly. On the eastern side of the path was a stone containing two large fissures; the northern fissure was where Rabbi Shimon had sat, and the southern one where Rabbi Abba had sat. At a nearby tree, facing these two clefts, Rabbi Elazar had been seated. The Ari seated himself within the northern fissure, as Rabbi Shimon had done before him, and I sat within the southern one, not knowing that this was the seat of Rabbi Abba. It was only after this encounter that my teacher explained to me the significance of what had taken place. Now I know what he had in mind when he told me that I contain the spark of one of the members of the Idra (assembly).

Anyone familiar with the writings of the Ari will realize that his clarity and depth of thought and understanding could only come from one blessed with the spirit of Rabbi Shimon. Only Rabbi Shimon's soul would have been capable of the feats of transcendence that are clearly indicated in the Ari's writings. Some people thought that the Ari was the harbinger of the Messianic Age, and an extraordinary legend grew up concerning his piety and righteousness. One *Erev Shabbat* (Sabbath eve) the Ari assembled his disciples and declared that he could effect the coming of the Messiah that very Shabbat. He stressed to all present the importance of complete harmony, warning them to be aware of the slightest confrontation with one another. So the unique Shabbat began, and all went well throughout Friday night and Shabbat morning. Towards the close of Shabbat, a trivial argument broke out among the children of the Ari's disciples. This quarrel escalated until the parents intervened, leading in turn to a disagreement among two of the disciples. Shabbat ended without the appearance of the Messiah; the disciples showed their disappointment at being unworthy of his coming, and asked their teacher the reason for this. The Ari replied sadly, "For a small pittance the arrival of the Messiah was forestalled." Little did his disciples know that Satan resorts to any means to divert men from their noble intentions. Knowing all too well the disciples' awareness of the important task of maintaining harmony among themselves, he chose a covert and unsuspected approach to gain his objective of disunity. "Thus," concluded the Ari, "the coming of the Messiah does not mean that we must wait for some individual to ride through the gate of Mercy in the Eastern Wall of the city of Jerusalem, mounted on a white donkey. Rather, the presence of goodwill towards men and peace on earth, as indicated in the verse 'The wolf shall dwell with the lamb, and the leopard shall lie down with the kid' (Isaiah 11:6), is the Messiah. The Messiah is nothing more than the symbol of world harmony". Hearing this, the disciples departed with bowed heads.

On another occasion the Ari gathered his disciples together for a journey to Jerusalem in order to spend Shabbat there. When they heard his intention they were overcome with bewilderment and asked their teacher how he could contemplate such a long journey when the arrival of the Shabbat was only a matter of minutes away. Smiling, the Ari replied, "The elements of time, space and motion are merely an expression of the limitations imposed by the physical body on the soul.

When the soul has sway over the body, however, these limiting factors cease to exist. Let us now proceed to Jerusalem, therefore, for our corporeal bodies have lost their influence over our souls". In this way, singing mystical chants, the Ari and his disciples arrived in Jerusalem in time to celebrate the coming of the Sabbath.

At the age of thirty-eight, on the fifth day of Av 1572, the Ari completed his task on earth and ascended to the place waiting for him in the Garden of Eden.

HAIM AND SHMUEL VITAL

Their relationship with the Ari — the "accidents" of history bring together the great minds of Kabbalah as part of the eternal scheme leading to redemption — the Ari's explanation of the purpose of his reincarnation — the exalted level of Haim Vital's spirit.

To his most trusted and favored pupil Haim Vital, and to Haim's son, Shmuel Vital, the Ari gave the task of recording his thoughts and teachings on paper as a record for posterity for the Golden Age of Kabbalah in Safed. These two devoted followers summarized, as far as was possible, the deeds and wisdom of their teacher, producing the volumes that we now regard as the Ari's writings. Haim Vital became a legendary figure and a source of wisdom for later Kabbalists, who could now refer to a concise and clear literary work that laid open the heretofore obscure and abstruse contents of the central work of Kabbalistic literature, the Zohar.

The faculty of human reason has alienated many people from the basic tenets of the Torah, due largely to the difficulty in accepting as intrinsic truths those teachings that are based on a literal understanding of the Law. A prime objective of the Ari's commentary was to present truth in a logical, consecutive manner. The system devised by Rabbi Shimon was not immediately apparent to students and scholars of the Kabbalah, leading some to claim that the knowledge of the *Book of Splendor* (the Zohar) was irrational and illogical. The writings of the Ari, however, refute this claim completely, pointing out that they represent a commentary on the Zohar that can be grasped by the intellect and perceived by the senses. Where ambiguous and figurative expressions and seemingly inconsequential stories in the Torah leave an impression of irrelevancy, the writings caution the reader to beware of literal interpretations. Where some aspect of Torah appears to contradict common sense, the Ari reminds us that the metaphors of the law were intended to enable the uneducated merely to comprehend to the best of their abilities. To the knowledgeable, a deeper interpretation of such stories should present itself. The parables themselves are of no great value until their inner, sublime meanings have been made intelligible by means of the study of the Kabbalah.

We have already seen that the "accidents" of history that brought together the great minds of Kabbalah in Safed, were, in fact, part of the eternal scheme leading to the eventual redemption of mankind. The presence of Haim and Shmuel Vital was a part of this unfolding, and is demonstrated by their unerring grasp of an enormous body of sublime Kabbalistic scholarship. They presented concepts that were not perceptible through the five senses and identified truths that could not be attained through the exercise of logic or imagination. The Ari himself implied that his reincarnation on this earth was largely for the purpose of instructing Ḥaim Vital in the mysteries of Kabbalah. Furthermore, his presence permitted Vital to rectify faults in the many reincarnated personalities that he contained — among them being Cain, Koraḥ, Yoḥanan ben Zakai and Rabbi Akiva.[72] In addition, the Ari told Vital that his soul contained sparks of the Divine Essence that were of a higher degree than those possessed by many of the supernal angels. "But more than that I may not reveal; if I were to reveal your essence to you, you would quite literally fly with joy, but I have not been granted permission to discuss your incarnation in greater detail."[73]

One Friday night Moses Alshikh — the most important homiletician of the 16th century — came to the Ari and asked him why he should receive the Ari's teachings only through Ḥaim Vital, who was considerably his junior. The Ari replied, "I have returned to this world solely for the purpose of teaching Ḥaim Vital, since no other student is capable of learning so much as a single letter from me."[74] When Vital himself put the same question to him, the Ari told him that the study of Kabbalah did not depend on the student's level of understanding, intelligence or active intellect, but rather on his spirit which is incarnated from a supernal level.[75] He told Vital that he would soon come face to face with the Prophet Elijah and talk of many things with him; also, that through repentance and good deeds, he would complete and amend his Nefesh (the Crude Spirit that represents the lowest level of the soul), and would ascend the ladder to a higher level of Ruaḥ (Spirit) which would ultimately unite with the Ruaḥ of Rabbi Akiva[76]

One Shabbat, the Ari noticed the following text on Ḥaim Vital's forehead: "They prepared a chair for Ḥezkiahu, King of Judah."[77] He understood immediately that a part of the soul of Ḥezkiahu had joined that of Ḥaim Vital through the mystery of

Tosefet Shabbat, whereby one acquires on Shabbat parts of other souls which may remain for a longer or shorter time, depending on the actions of the recipient. During that Shabbat Vital became angry with a member of his family, and the additional soul consequently left him. After a week of repentance, the Ari noticed on the following Shabbat the embodiment of the Ruah, or higher level of soul, of both Hezkiahu and Rabbi Akiva in Haim Vital. Having thus attained a majestic level of spirituality, Vital was unable to prevent the influence of the left column from distracting him from his path of piety — again he quarreled with members of his family, and again the spirits of Hezkiahu and Rabbi Akiva left him. This time, however, he repented immediately and emended the entire left column of anger, whereupon Ben Azzai, the son-in-law of Rabbi Akiva, entered his spiritual realm.[78]

The Ari considered it necessary to reveal Haim Vital's levels of spirituality to him in this way in order to explain why his exalted vessel had been chosen and prepared to receive the great light that would illumine the sublime wisdom of Kabbalah. One day Vital asked the Ari, "How can you tell me that my soul is so elevated when it is well known that even the pious of former generations were of such a high degree of elevation that I can never hope to reach even their comparatively low level of spirituality?" The Ari replied, "The levels of spirituality are not dependent on Man's deeds or incarnated soul alone, but are in relation to the level of the generation in which he finds himself; thus a minor deed in our generation may be compared to much greater deeds in previous generations, due to the severity and dominance of the *klipot* (the shells or vessels of Evil) in the world today. Had you lived in an earlier time, therefore, these same deeds of yours would have been superior to those of the most pious of that generation. This is similar to what has been said with regard to Noah:

that he was righteous in his wicked generation (Genesis 6:9); had he lived in a generation of righteous men, he would certainly have been a more righteous individual. You should not, therefore, be amazed or confused about your exalted spiritual level."[79]

On another occasion, when Vital implored the Ari to tell him why he did not devote his valuable time to more eminent scholars such as Yosef Caro, the Radbaz, the Ari's teacher, or the Alshikh, the Ari replied, "Do I really need you? Do I derive any benefit from my association with you? On the contrary, your extreme youth, compared with those scholars that you mentioned, should give me reason to associate more closely with them, so that my reputation might be enhanced; if that were my objective, I would certainly have chosen that way. However, after considering the matter carefully, and reflecting upon these righteous persons, penetrating their innermost recesses, I find no vessel as pure and as spiritually elevated as yours. This should satisfy your curiosity; I have no intention of revealing the secrets of these men, and you should rather rejoice in your share of the spiritual realm."[80]

So it was that Haim Vital and his son Shmuel labored together to produce the Writings of the Ari. Shmuel recorded every word transmitted to him by his father with the efficiency of an accomplished scribe, and the resulting volumes achieved great fame as the classic textbook on the Zohar.

Now just as in the case of his father Haim Vital, Shmuel Vital had also been carefully chosen to perform the tasks allocated to him in his lifetime.

SPIRITUAL DEVELOPMENT OF THE KABBALAH

If we are to understand the significance of the doctrines of Kabbalah in our own times, it is important to have some understanding of the spiritual development of the Kabbalah in past ages. The characters and personalities of the Kabbalists of Safed were the channels or cables through which the power of the Kabbalah was transmitted, since complete understanding of its wisdom is impossible unless we are aware of the spiritual composition of those who taught it, or those who set it down for future generations. This is made possible through the sublime teachings of Rabbi Shimon, later developed and elaborated upon by the Ari, regarding the transmigration of the soul.

In the *Sefer haGilgulim* (the Book of Transmigrations), the Ari describes the developments leading to the exile and migration of Shmuel Vital's soul and their significance in relation to the mission to which he was assigned during his life on earth. According to the Ari, there were special affinities between Haim Vital and his son. Haim's first wife was a reincarnation of Kalba Savua, Rabbi Akiva's father-in-law; because her soul had its origins in a male, she could not bear children. As the Ari explained, [81]

> And Hannah will die, and you (Haim) will marry again when your Nefesh (lower aspect of the soul) is corrected, and you join the second level of the spiritual ladder, which is the Ruah. When your Nefesh has enveloped that of Rabbi Akiva, your Ruah will become joined to his, and only then will you be permitted to marry your true soulmate. She will be on the same spiritual plane as Rabbi Akiva's soulmate, since your soul and that of Rabbi Akiva

are truly united on the levels of Nefesh and Ruaḥ. Then you will marry Kalba Savua's daughter Rachel, and will be blessed with a son, whom you will call Shmuel.

So far it is clear that Shmuel Vital's spiritual background was of the rarest quality; however, there is as yet no indication of why he was chosen for the specific task of recording the teachings of the Ari as they were reported to him by his father. For this information, we must turn to Ḥaim Vital himself.

One day Ḥaim Vital revealed to his son that he was a reincarnation of Rabbi Meir, the celebrated *Tannah*. Later Shmuel had a dream in which the Rabbi himself told him the same. It is stated in the *Mishnah* that Rabbi Meir was the foremost scribe of his generation. Rabbi Joseph Vital, Ḥaim Vital's grandfather, was also blessed with a spark of the soul of Rabbi Meir, and he too was a noted scribe. Ḥaim Vital says of his grandfather that he was one of the greatest scribes the world has ever known. "The Ari told me," he said to his son, "that at one time half the world received spiritual nourishment through the merits of our grandfather, because of the accuracy and faithfulness with which, in his position as scribe, he prepared the written portion of *Tefillin*. You, my son, are incarnated with that spark as well, which is why you are able to record the works of the Ari with such accuracy."[82]

Shmuel Vital was ideally suited to his task, as indeed, were his father Ḥaim Vital and their teacher, the Ari. Through the spiritual vessel of Shmuel the world was now prepared to enter the Messianic era, fully equipped with all the necessary material and knowledge to carry out the work required of it; however, despite the fact that a complete commentary on the Zohar was now available, the metaphors and interwoven imagery were still understood only by a select few.

While it is true to say that the Lurianic system provides the necessary background for a full and comprehensive understanding of the Zohar, it is nonetheless puzzling that Haim Vital should have almost totally ignored the commentaries of the master Kabbalist, Moses Cordovero, the Ari's mentor. According to legend the reason lies in a dream that Haim Vital once had, in which Moses Cordovero appeared before him and told him that, although both his system and that of the Ari were correct interpretations of the Zohar, the Ari's would prevail in the Messianic era. This, in fact, is the case today, when the Writings of the Ari have been arranged, organized and published, while those of the Ramak (Rabbi Moses Cordovero) have only recently been discovered.

ABRAHAM BEN MORDEKHAI AZULAI

> *Born to a family of Kabbalists — his writings of three treatises on the Zohar — he urges the study of the Kabbalah to hasten the appearance of the Messiah*

Another famous Kabbalist who flourished during the Golden Age of Enlightenment, which lasted from about 1490 until 1590, was Abraham ben Mordekhai Azulai (1570-1643). Born in Fez to a family of Kabbalists of Castilian origin, he wrote three treatises based on the Zohar: *Or haLevanah* (Light of the Moon), *Or haHamah* (Light of the Sun), and *Or haGanuz* (the Hidden Light), all three being based primarily on the Lurianic system. He also prepared a volume entitled *Hesed l'Avraham* (Mercy of Abraham), in which he presented an analysis of the principles of Kabbalah.

The work of his preface to *Or haHamah* ring with greater force today than ever before. "It is most important from this time on that everyone study the Kabbalah publicly and preoccupy themselves with it. For, by the merit of Kabbalah — in fact, solely through Kabbalah — the Messiah will appear and forever efface war, destruction, social injustice and, above all, man's inhumanity to his fellow man."

THE GOLDEN AGE OF ENLIGHTENMENT

It may be said, therefore, that the Spanish Inquisition, for all its violence, ushered in the Golden Age of Enlightenment, and that the Lurianic era set the stage for the Messianic age.

8

A LATER LIGHT
RABBI YEHUDAH ASHLAG

WRITINGS

*The pioneering work of A Study of the Ten
Luminous Emanations renews interest in
Kabbalah — translates the Zohar into modern Hebrew making the Hebrew more comprehensible — his knowledge in every known
science is demonstrated in his writings*

DESPITE THE GROWTH AND INFLUENCE OF HASIDISM WITH ITS
renewed interest in Kabbalah, it would still be true to say that
the majority of Jews remained as ignorant of the teachings of
Kabbalah as ever. This situation began to change, however,
when Rabbi Yehudah Ashlag (1886-1955) pioneered a new
system for understanding the works of the Ari. In his sixteen-
volume textbook, the *Study of the Ten Luminous Emanations*

(Talmud Eser haSfirot) he devised a logical system through which the essence of the transcendent realm was transmitted by means of an array of symbols and illustrations. These, he felt, best described those aspects of the teachings of the Ari that were beyond the grasp of the intellect alone. The *Ten Luminous Emanations* deals with those concepts that have eluded the most determined scholars for centuries. The intimate relationship between the physical and metaphysical realms is presented simply, together with a description of the series of evolutions that culminate in the world we know today, and also a detailed presentation of those motives that may be ascribed to the Creator.

In addition to these volumes, Rabbi Ashlag's monumental work on the Zohar has had a great influence on Judaic studies and marks a turning point in the attempt to render the Kabbalah comprehensible to contemporary students. His was the first translation of the entire Zohar into modern Hebrew. Realizing that a comprehensive translation would not be sufficient on its own, he also composed a commentary on the most difficult passages, and compiled a volume of diagrams describing the process of the evolution of the *Sfirot* in all their manifestations down to the level of this world.

Generally speaking, Kabbalists of the rank and stature of Rabbi Ashlag receive their knowledge through Divine revelation. They tend to be men with a broad rabbinic education, and Rabbi Ashlag was no exception in this respect. More penetrating, however, was his knowledge of the spectrum of Kabbalah, and his translation of the Zohar shows clearly that he was knowledgeable in every known science.

LIFE HISTORY

Born in Warsaw and educated in Hasidic schools he emigrates to Palestine — well versed in the field of metaphysics and closely connected with the higher levels — his influence on the expansion of scientific theory

I was told of Rabbi Ashlag's life and personality by my Master Rabbi Yehudah Z. Brandwein, who was his disciple. Rabbi Ashlag was born in Warsaw and educated in Hasidic schools. In his early years, he was a student of Shalom Rabinowitz of Kalushin and of his son Yehoshua Asher of Porissor. He emigrated to Palestine in 1919 and settled in the Old City of Jerusalem. Rabbi Brandwein spoke of him as a man with immense powers of meditation, a man to whom the world of metaphysics and mysticism were as familiar as was the world of physics to Einstein. The comparison is not altogether without significance, since it was during Rabbi Ashlag's lifetime that great advances and discoveries were being made in the world of science, destroying many of the traditional scientific theories of stability, permanence and purpose in the universe. The great monument of that scientific era, Einstein's Theory of Relativity, confirmed what Kabbalists had known to be true for centuries — that time, space and motion are not immutable constants but a function of energy.

The increasing awareness among scientists of the shortcomings of the analytic methodology of science and the growing sense of the unity and interrelatedness of physical and biological systems have given a fresh impetus to the world of mysticism, and particularly to Kabbalah. In this respect, the works of

Rabbi Ashlag are distinguished by their unique and striking mixture of salient facts concerning the structure of the universe, together with a deep, penetrating description of the purpose of the individual within this system.

The restoration of a mystical approach in the world of Kabbalah, as opposed to the dry study of ritual and ceremony for its own sake, draws a large part of its strength from the link between the concepts expressed by the author and his mystical consciousness. Since the beginnings of Kabbalah the Prophet Elijah has been closely identified with its profound teachings. He appeared to both Rabbi Shimon and the Ari. Rabbi Ashlag, however, did not claim Elijah as the source of his mystical revelation. A beautiful story told to me by my master, Rabbi Brandwein, demonstrates the inner connection that existed between the soul of Rabbi Ashlag and the levels on high. "One evening," recalled Rabbi Ashlag, "following the completion of a volume of the Zohar, I dozed off into a very deep slumber. A voice came to me and proclaimed that I would be shown the entire Creation, from the beginning to the very end, including the coming of the Messiah. I then asked why I could not be shown that which the prophets had seen. The reply was, 'Why should you be satisfied with the visionary level of the prophets, when you can see it all?'"

The source of his revelation is described in a letter written by Rabbi Ashlag to an uncle,[83] in which he related his meeting with his master, and the aura of egocentricity that he assumed after learning the inner mysteries of the Kabbalah. This element of pride led his master to discontinue the lessons until Rabbi Ashlag had adopted the correct attitude of humility, whereupon his master — a stranger whose name he was forbidden to utter — revealed to him a *Sod* (a secret or inner meaning) concerning the *Mikveh* (ritual bath). "This," reports

Rabbi Ashlag, "brought on an ecstasy of such intensity that it literally created a total *Dvekut,* a cleaving to the Divine Essence, a complete separation from corporeality, and a tearing asunder of the veil of eternal life." Shortly after this revelation his master passed away, leaving him brokenhearted. As a result of his deep sorrow and despair the revelation, too, left him for a while, until he was once more able to devote his life to the Creator, "... whereupon the fountains of heavenly wisdom suddenly burst forth, [and] with the grace of the Almighty, I remembered all the revelations I had received from my master, of blessed memory."

Today, as in the Golden Age of Safed, the invisible spring of Kabbalah has once again come to the surface. In our times, however, we notice one significant difference — science, for so long the sworn enemy of all religion, can now be seen in its true light as the ally and companion of Kabbalah.

9

KABBALAH AND
THE AGE OF THE MESSIAH

WHY WAS THE ZOHAR
CONCEALED IN THE PAST?

LET US LOOK IN GREATER DETAIL AT THE APPROPRIATENESS of the study of Kabbalah at this time; in particular, the connection between the study of Kabbalah and the approach of the Messianic Age.

We have already observed the rising tide of interest in occult teachings and in the Zohar, and the reawakening of spirituality within Judaism and other religions. The question is then raised why the Zohar was effectively concealed from earlier generations, since they were undoubtedly at a more conscious and spiritual level than our own and thus better equipped to understand the Kabbalah's profound wisdom.

THE VIEW OF THE TALMUD

*A paradox explained — relying on writings,
later generations discover and explore the
Zohar — the Desire to Receive lets in the
Light Force, the highest power*

Discussions in the Talmud anticipate the questions being raised in this generation. It is concerned with the nature of spirituality and its change over the span of time. In their discussions the sages show that they are fully aware of the paradox at the center of the issue; the earlier generations, being more spiritual by nature, needed less in the way of spiritual knowledge from books, yet achieved more in the realm of working wonders and miracles. Thus we find a situation in which it appears that greater knowledge and more intensive study is less rewarded. The resolution of this paradox lies in the spiritual level achieved in different generations. The earlier generations were, quite simply, closer to the source of spirituality than are the later ones; they demanded far less from the physical world — both physically and spiritually, they were on a higher plane of existence. Being thus less dependent on the mundane vessels of the physical world, they could maintain their elevated status, and indeed exert control over the direction of the world, through their spirituality. The expression of this control was the manifestation of "miracles", meaning the display of their power over the natural order of the universe. Later generations have to rely to a greater extent on knowledge from secondary sources, such as the written word. At the same time, their greater dependence on the world — their Desire to Receive — makes them more capable of receiving the Light, which is of the highest nature. The vessels to receive that Light are of a coarser material, but the Light, once it has penetrated, is present in a much more explicit form than in former generations. Instead of one book — six books. Instead of just Mishnah — Talmud. Instead of just Talmud — Zohar.

Part Three

MAKING THE CONNECTION, PRACTICAL APPLICATIONS

Every day below is controlled by a day above.
Now an act below stimulates a corresponding activity above.
Thus, if a man does kindness on earth,
he awakens loving kindness above,
and it rests upon that day which
is crowned therewith through him.
Similarly, if he performs a deed of mercy,
he crowns that day with mercy and
it becomes his protector in the hour of need.

Zohar III, P.92a

10

OPERATIONAL TOOLS

ALTHOUGH THE KABBALAH DEALS WITH MATTERS OF AN ELE-vated spiritual nature, it does so with the sole intention of providing one with tools of a high enough quality for one to fulfill one's own potential. The teachings of Kabbalah are not intended to be confined to the realms of abstract thought processes or disciplines learned for the sake of discipline alone, but should lead directly to the application of those elevated thoughts and methods of learning in the realm of action.

MITZVOT

> *The mitzvot and commandments of the Torah*
> *are eternally relevant*

A Kabbalistic analysis of the *mitzvot* and the command-ments of the Torah gives one an immediate insight into the essence of the physical level, by demonstrating how the eternal laws of the universe manifest themselves in our material world. Those people who regard the precepts as outmoded or irrelevant are ignorant of their true nature, which is that of conduits or cables through which the profound wisdom of the Creator, and the metaphysical laws and principles of the universe, are revealed.

The Zohar, sensing that the *mitzvot* are profound symbols filled with priceless and unguessed treasures, goes far beyond the customary approaches to knowledge, as we shall see.

THE WISDOM OF THE KABBALAH

> *Kabbalah reveals the unchanging truth contained in the Torah — each* mitzvah *has its own significance and function — dogmatic approach to observance is not found in Kabbalah — true religion as a path shared with us by the sages of the past — the religious person defined*

In explaining the significance and function of each *mitzvah*, philosophical discourses that do not have a basis in the sublime and eternal wisdom of the Kabbalah are bound to lead to divergent or even opposing points of view, whereas the root knowledge contained in Kabbalah reveals the eternal nature of the unchanging truth that is contained in every word of Torah. The Kabbalistic attitude towards fulfillment of these precepts does not reflect a dogmatic approach requiring the individual to demonstrate his or her allegiance to the Lord by adhering rigorously to the confines of strict obedience. There are many areas, the Kabbalah tells us, where our feeble mental capacity is totally unable to grasp the understanding of the mysteries of the universe and of its Creator, but within these limitations there are also many aspects of our world that are revealed through knowledge of the workings of the metaphysical realm.

True religion is a path along which the seeker no longer gropes in blindness and fear; it is a path that has been trodden in the full light of wisdom by the sages of the past, who have foreseen the problems and pitfalls that would face the novice, and have shared their knowledge with us so that their example may be a light for future generations. True religion deals with the firm principles and laws of the universe, cognizant of the fact that any deviation from that path might result in physical as well as emotional disturbances. It can be regarded as the system of laws which governs and generates the physical and ethical laws of the world we live in. The religious man thus becomes one who has knowledge of the workings of this higher system and of its applications and implications in the lower physical world.

In each of the six hundred and thirteen *mitzvot* there is an underlying reason — not just an outward sign of devotion, but an instruction regarding the usefulness or danger of some aspect of the universe. Whereas the Torah and Talmud give us a general idea of the nature of these aspects, only the Kabbalah reveals their true identity as tools with which we can work to achieve the goal of union with the Creator. The *mitzvot* exist in order to enable us to keep a balance in the universal forces of energy that resulted from the Creation.[84] The ultimate balance, we learn from Hillel, which is the ultimate *mitzvah,* is the relationship between a man and his fellow, guided at all times by the principle of "love your neighbor as yourself". The rest, indeed, is commentary.

THE TOOL SUGGESTED BY HILLEL

> *Love your neighbor as yourself — a guide to*
> *the final goal of self-improvement — culti-*
> *vating the Desire to Impart — drawing*
> *closer to the Creator*

The Kabbalistic philosophy regarding Divine command-ments and rituals is best described by the legend of Hillel. According to this legend, a recent convert to Judaism came before Hillel and asked him if it was possible to teach the entire Torah while standing on one leg. Hillel replied, "That which is hateful to you, do not do unto your neighbor. This is the entire Torah. The remaining decrees and commandments are but a commentary on this basic principle."[85]

The convert's request refers to the ultimate objectives of Torah — the termination of the path along which deeds and service lead. The entire content of the Torah, its laws and commandments, are nothing more than instruments for the improvement and development of self-control. Therefore Hillel chose the one precept of "love your neighbor" as the specific idea that can guide man to this final goal. The precept reveals the inner spirituality of the individual, the incarnation of the truly Divine within him, and thus draws him closer to the source of Light and beauty. This source, which we have called the Desire to Impart, is the chief characteristic by which we can come to know the Creator.

We learn from the Book of Genesis that the "inclination of man's heart is evil from his youth."[86] This refers to the essence of man, the Desire to Receive, which until the age of religious majority dominates all actions in the guise of a Desire to Receive for oneself alone. The actions of a child are motivated by this essence, without any regard for others and without any Desire to Impart to anyone else.

Upon reaching the age of Bar or Bat Mitzvah — thirteen years for a boy, twelve for a girl — the individual is incarnated with a *Yetzer haTov*, a good inclination, which is a potential metaphysical form of energy similar to the Creator's Desire to Impart. From that age onwards, the concept of "Love your neighbor" becomes the link connecting all that exists in the celestial heights with the lower level of this world. Man is the channel through which the Creator's beneficence and grace flow from the upper heavenly spheres to the corporeal world. The degree and intensity of this union, however, depends on the extent to which human egocentricity transforms itself into the Desire to Impart, since the nature of a channel or cable is to transmit energy, not to absorb it. We can compare this to the result of placing a curtain in front of the light of the sun: the thicker the curtain, representing the Desire to Receive, the more the light will absorb into itself, while a thin curtain will present less obstruction to the passage of the light. It should be clear from this example that the thinner curtain has a greater affinity for the original source of light — the sun. Although the thin curtain has no light of its own, it nonetheless has an aspect of the Desire to Impart (which is also the essential quality of light), in that it does not hinder the passage of the light. The thick curtain, on the other hand, through its absorption of light, takes on the opposite characteristic, the Desire to Receive, thus bringing about a separation of function between it and the sun.

If the identity of function is the final destination of the soul — the intimate and permanent union resulting from the conformity of Divine and human wills — then we must direct our attention to the words of our Talmudic sages concerning the Evil Inclination. The Creator, in addressing Himself to the human will, declares, "I created an evil inclination, and also the Torah with its commandments and rituals as a means for the transformation of the evil inclination." Torah study and observance of its precepts gradually nurture the individual until he or she is sufficiently disciplined to remove all traces of this "love of oneself only", so that all deeds are sanctified by a desire to impart to others. The ethical and moral commandments that apply between man and his neighbor secure for the individual the structure of the aspect of selflessness which is implied by the concept of "love your neighbor".

We can therefore understand the words of Hillel to the convert more profoundly: by achieving the goal of loving our neighbor, we are transforming our inherent Desire to Receive for ourselves only (which separates us from the Creator) into the Desire to Impart, which, through its identity of form with the Creator's imparting aspect, draws us closer to Him and thus fulfills the original thought of Creation.

11

DVEKUT - THE CIRCULAR CONCEPT

THE UNION OF UPPER AND LOWER, THE BRINGING TOGETHER of opposites, brings us full circle in the chain of metaphysical events by which the universe is structured.

UNION WITH THE CREATOR

> *The spiritual force of the Creator: to impart*
> *— the spiritual force of mankind: desire to*
> *receive — union with the Creator, bringing*
> *together the spiritual forces — dealing with*
> *the instinct of self-reliance*

The union of man and his Creator is known as Dvekut, or cleaving. Union with the Creator is fundamentally a bringing together of metaphysical entities. Just as the separation or union of tangible objects is accomplished by either removing them from each other or by bringing one part closer to the other in space, so it is with metaphysical or spiritual forces. Separation or union is achieved through the transformation of contrasting phases which either sever or unite.

The Creator is, as we have said, purely a bestower; He imparts without being in any way diminished by imparting and receives nothing in return. In this, he is the measure of the perfect donor. Mankind, on the contrary, has a perpetual and unfilled craving for the fulfillment of its needs and desires, due to its eternal Desire to Receive; this is the vital intention within the Thought of Creation. The Desire to Receive is thus both a mark of man's essence and also the cause of the separation of his being from that of the Creator. This chasm is widened when man perceives himself as being a receptacle for his own benefit alone, when his vessel attempts to capture and contain the Light with no thought of sharing or imparting it to others. Thus, while his natural instinct is towards self-reliance rather than reliance on others, he is still aware through the influence of his consciousness that he is very much reliant on the bounty of the Creator.

BALANCING RECEIVING AND SHARING

Receiving the Creator's bounty to fulfill the thought of Creation — know the correct way to receive and give

This awareness of reliance on the bounty of the Creator may lead to the conclusion that receiving the Creator's beneficence is only for the purpose of rendering delight to the Creator.

The two alternatives — receiving purely for oneself or accepting the Creator's beneficence in order to share with others and thus rendering Him great delight — are mutually exclusive. It would appear that we are caught in a trap, for by putting ourselves at the mercy of the Creator's bounty, we experience Bread of Shame because we have received something for nothing and rely on that which we have not earned. This, the Zohar teaches, is the complete opposite of what in fact happens. By accepting the Creator's beneficence, we are fulfilling not only the role of our own individual creation, but also of the original Thought of Creation. This can happen only if we are aware of the correct way in which to give and to receive. This, as we have said, is the purpose of Kabbalah, which literally means Receiving. In the balanced relationship between donor and recipient, the aspect of Bread of Shame is rendered void, since we have created a situation in which, although there is giving and taking, there is equal measure on both sides, so that there is no feeling of lack or shame.

We find this idea elaborated in a treatise of the Talmud regarding the laws of the marriage ceremony.[87] It is specified that during the ceremony the man is required to present a wedding ring to his bride, by which exchange she becomes his legal wife. This is the Mosaic law, and the reasons supporting it will be considered more fully in a volume on the concept of soulmates, marriage and divorce. The Talmud, however, cites one occasion where the traditional order of the marriage ceremony is reversed. When the bridegroom is a man of great merit, due to the study of Torah, the bride may give the wedding ring to him, instead of he to her, and on his reciting the traditional formula, "you shall by this become betrothed to me", she then becomes his legal wife. The Talmud explains that "through his recipiency, the marriage has become legalized by her delight in being honored by his acceptance of the ring, although the legal procedure has been reversed."[88]

In most marriages the *Halakha* is followed, and the man gives a material token (a ring or coin) as symbol of marriage.[89] The important point to note here is that the significance of his act is the giving, the token ring or coin being of no intrinsic value. However, in the exceptional case we have described, we are forced to conclude that the bridegroom's act of receiving the ring from his bride is in itself regarded as an act of giving. Instead of giving her a coin or ring, which is a material symbol, he presents her with the far more lofty and spiritual delight of honoring her by marriage. Receiving that is undertaken for the sole purpose of imparting constitutes absolute, complete bestowal. Thus the groom in this instance is considered by the sages of the Talmud to be giving more by receiving the ring than he would if he were to give it. In the case of the Godly man his very marriage is an act of giving, so that the ring, the symbol of consummation, is passed from woman to man. There is also an equivalent heightening in the transference of spiritiual energy, since by her act of giving, the bride is receiving and, more to the point, she is receiving far more than she would have done had she merely received the ring from the man. In this heightened dynamic interchange of energy, the relationship is consummated, and the Bread of Shame is totally banished. Indeed, one might argue that the reversal of the normal marriage procedure when the groom is especially learned, since if this were not the case, the bride would be only receiving and would therefore be susceptible to the Bread of Shame. However, when she gives the ring to the man, she elevates her role of recipient to that of donor, and brings the necessary balance to the relationship.

There is a tale told by Kabbalists which illustrates this initially confusing concept clearly. The tale concerns a certain wealthy man who invited a number of friends to join him on some festive occasion. Just as the company was about to sit down to the festive meal, the host noticed a poor man passing by. He felt sorry for the man and instructed one of the servants to invite him in. All the guests could see that the poor man was badly in need of food and clothing, yet when the host cordially invited him to join them and share the meal, they were astonished to hear him refuse. The host, bewildered and mystified by the unexpected reply, urged the poor man to reconsider, only to be told that he (the poor man) had no need for this sort of charity. The host insisted, the poor man politely refused, and so the conversation continued until the poor man finally threw his hands in the air in a gesture of helplessness and said, "Very well, if it really means that much to you, I'll accept your kind hospitality." With a sigh of relief, the company sat down to begin the festivities.

In this story as in the example of the special marriage, the roles of donor and recipient are reversed, resutling in a heightening and sanctification of the transaction. To the receiver — the poor man — the request that he receive beneficence without due regard to his having earned this kindness appears initially as something degrading: this is identical to the concept of Bread of Shame. Thus what appeared to be simple generosity on the part of the host takes on a new aspect in the light of the poor man's inability to share or impart anything and so remove the Bread of Shame. It emerges as something unwanted — not because the poor man is not in need of food, but because there is no way in which he can take it as yet without losing his self-respect. Faced with the choice between humiliation and hunger, it is perhaps no longer surprising that he refuses the food. A receiver who is not prepared to share or who is prevented from sharing will inevitably reject the true intention of the donor. This built-in metaphysical rejection became inevitable after the initial feeling of Bread of Shame was experienced by the souls in the world of *Ein Sof.*

However, once this unexpected refusal of an obviously desired gift has taken place, the flow of energy in the situation begins to change. The rich man realizes that he has been deprived of an opportunity to do good, and begins to become more insistent and pleading. In effect, he is now no longer offering the poor man food by asking him a favor — that he afford him the opportunity of sharing some of his wealth, and of receiving pleasure from that sharing. The poor man now experiences a situation where he is being asked to impart as well as receive and therefore consents to join the feast. The rich man, too, is both giving and receiving. The cycle has been completed, with flow and feedback now in a state of dynamic balance.

We can apply this example to any form of benenvolence; unless there is this balance between donor and receiver, the original intention of the donor will not be realized. This holds true on all levels, beginning with the original Thought of Creation which was to impart Ineffable Goodness to man, and which will be realized finally only when we have learned how to properly receive and interact on the level of family, friendship and business.

THE CIRCULAR CONCEPT

Circular concept bound up with the individual soul and all souls — a path of life uniting

> *the realm of metaphysics with earthly reality*
> *— social intercourse and commitment to*
> *society — through diversity we remove the*
> *aspect of Bread of Shame — the transmuta-*
> *tion of our elemental characteristic (Desire*
> *to Receive) into the fundamental characteris-*
> *tic of the Creator (to Impart) — attaining*
> *Dvekut with Hillel's tool — the virtue of*
> *Dvekut, union with the Creator*

The foregoing analysis reveals the fundamental necessity for this "circular concept". It is bound up not only with the redemption of the individual soul, but also with the redemption of all souls that are associated with the age of the Messiah. Through the circular concept, it becomes possible to convert the Desire to Receive into a Desire to Impart, transmuting, we might say, the letter M in "me" to the letter W in "we"; the "M" points downwards, emphasizing the connection with the physical world, while the "W" reaches up towards the Heavens, indicating its affinity for the concept of *Dvekut*, or communion with the Creator.

Through this affinity of desires, we are brought closer to the structure of the Creator's Desire to Impart and can free ourselves from the stigma of being able to receive only for ourselves. From our earthly existence we are led to a higher spiritual level of consciousness, to a liberation from the tyranny of the five senses, and to a higher realm of spiritual existence.

Dvekut, in Kabbalistic terms, is a profound concept but by no means unattainable. Love of man — or for that matter, love of the Creator — is not merely a mystical or theological concept, but rather a path of life through which the realm of metaphysics can be permanently united with earthly reality, thus liberating the true spiritual nature of man. It is not a teaching of austerity or asceticism, against which the sages often warned. One is not required to relinquish all the material possessions and physical comforts that are associated with corporeal existence in order to achieve spiritual growth. Indeed, *Dvekut* is realized within the framework of the physical world more effectively through social intercourse and commitment to society than by seclusion and self-denial, as Hillel implied in his answer to the convert.

In working toward the ultimate objective of *Dvekut*, the gradual transformation of receiving for oneself into receiving in order to share, those precepts between man and man are more likely to lead one to the goal by reason of one's ever-changing role and position in the daily demands of existence. The differentiation of desires that we find in our dealings with those around us forces us to explore in real terms the meaning of "love your neighbor," and to recognize the diversity that has existed since the *Ein Sof*. Through this diversity we shall eventually remove the aspect of Bread of Shame and return to the Blessed Endless.

In the process of spiritual elevation, each person is obliged to express his innermost potential of giving (and therefore, as we have understood, of receiving also), so as to achieve his own elevation, which permits the ultimate measure of beneficence and fulfillment from the Creator. Stated in simple terms, the precepts that regulate the interactions of men are the ideal conditioning agents for transforming man's basic character. These precepts are designed specifically to realign the selfish aspect of desire with the intention of the Creator, Whose fundamental characteristic is that of imparting.

This, then, is the core of Hillel's reply. "Love your neighbor" is, quite simply, the principal and most effective means of attaining *Dvekut*, which is the goal and purpose of Torah. The unifying force of this love, through which the individual may discover and draw on the innermost potential of his own positive qualities, assures the continuing progress of human development, inasmuch as the Desire to Receive has been kept in check.

The literal meaning of *Dvekut* reveals the very essence of man's relationship with the Creator and his fellow man. It implies attachment, a cleaving of two; while appearing to be a complete unit, each retains their individual characteristics. The Torah uses the same root to describe the relationship between a man and a woman, a union which is considered as making both parties whole, in that each brings what is lacking from the other to the relationship. *Dvekut* is derived from *devek* which is the root of *l'hidavek* (meaning "to attach"). It is used to portray this relationship between man and woman, as well as Man's union with the Creator.

Thus we find in the concept of *Dvekut* a central virtue by which each individual, and thus mankind as a whole, can reach Man's objective in this world, that of transmuting the elemental characteristic of Man into the fundamental characteristic of the Creator.

12

A CONTEMPLATION

A SYSTEM OF DEEDS AND DEVOTION

ALTHOUGH THE KNOWLEDGE OF KABBALAH IS DISCUSSED and encased in many volumes of writing, both ancient and modern, it should not be thought that its teachings are contained solely in the written word. In previous chapters we have shown that Kabbalah lies at the very heart of the system of holy actions and deeds known as *mitzvot*; without these actions, life is considered incomplete and lacking. However, inner devotion is also an important element of Jewish teaching, and this aspect, too, is emphasized by the teaching of Kabbalah.

KAVANNAH

The need to center one's inner world with the intention appropriate to the situation is known in Hebrew as *kavannah*, or Direction. While this meditation and the fulfillment of *mitzvot* are essentially inseparable, we feel that the reader who may have grown up without knowing the taste of *mitzvot*, will benefit from a contemplation to help link the teachings of Kabbalah with their application to the world of action. For this reason it seems fitting to close this book with a contemplation which, although no substitute for the performance of *mitzvot*, will, it is hoped, arouse in the reader a deeper appreciation of the intentions of this book, and allow him or her a further insight into the workings and significance of the teachings of Kabbalah.

THE METAPHOR OF THE BURNING CANDLE

The three elements of the flame of a candle and its symbolic meaning.

In the Zohar[90] we find a discussion of the two verses of Torah, "For the Lord your Creator is a consuming fire" (Deuter. 4:24), and "But you who did cleave unto the Lord your Creator are alive everyone of you this day" (Deuter. 4:4). The apparent contradiction in these words is explained by Rabbi Shimon:

> It has already been established that there is a fire which consumes and destroys, there being fires of different grades of strength. If we extend this concept, we might say that anyone wishing to penetrate the mystery of the holy unity should examine the flame that rises from a burning coal or candle.
>
> The flame cannot rise unless it is attached to some physical substance. Furthermore, within the flame itself there are to be found two lights: one is white

and luminous, the other black, or blue. The white light is the more elevated of the two and ascends steadily. The black or blue light is beneath and acts as a pedestal for the white light. The two are inseparably joined to one another, with the white light resting and enthroned upon the blue. The blue lower flame is itself attached to something physical beneath it, which feeds it and makes it join with the white flame above. Sometimes the blue light may become red in color, but the white light above never changes. Thus, the lower light, which is either blue or red, forms a connection between the white light above and the physical substance below, which keeps it alight. The nature of this lower light is to destroy anything that is beneath it or in contact with it; it is the source of destruction and death, nor does it ever change...This is why Moses said, "For the Lord your Creator is a consuming fire", meaning that He consumes all that is beneath Him — "*your Creator*" and not "*our Creator*", because Moses had reached the level of the upper white light, which does not consume or destroy.

The three elements that we can observe in the flame — the wick, the blue light and the white light — symbolize the three elements of man's spirit, and refer to the three columns we have discussed throughout this book. The white light represents the right column, the Desire to Impart; this is the moral strength which constantly strives to ascend to and unite with the Absolute. While it burns it does not consume, acting rather as an illuminating vehicle permeated with light through which an individual can become one with the eternal source of light, the Creator.

The blue or black flame symbolizes the left column, the Desire to Receive, and is characterized by its connection with the physical body. It constantly draws up energy from that which is beneath it, and represents the aspect of man that seeks to deny spirituality, pursuing material pleasures for oneself alone. Finally, the wick represents the synthesizing and unifying force of both the blue and the clear white flame, which is the central column.

If we draw only on the energy of the physical world, as the wick draws its energy from the body of the candle, that energy will, in time, be exhausted by the fire of the left column, the Desire to Receive. If, however, we connect with the limitless energy of the Creator, through a true understanding of the teachings of the Torah and a fulfillment of *mitzvot*, then we shall have transcended the destroying influence of the blue flame, and can connect with the unchanging purity of the clear white flame above. As we have stressed repeatedly throughout this book, this unity is not a negation of the left column, any more than the candle can burn without the blue flame. The choice facing us is whether to cut ourselves off from that endless source of energy and be consumed by the devouring fire of the Desire to Receive, or to connect with our birthright and cleave to the Creator without being destroyed.

The teachings of Kabbalah are not merely concerned, therefore, with theoretical descriptions of the structure of the universe. They are primarily concerned with preparing man for knowledge of the Almighty through direct awareness of the physical world, and through intuitive connections brought about by a deep contemplation of the relationships between the upper and lower worlds.

APPENDICES

APPENDIX 1
The Tree Of Life

THE UPPER TRIANGLE

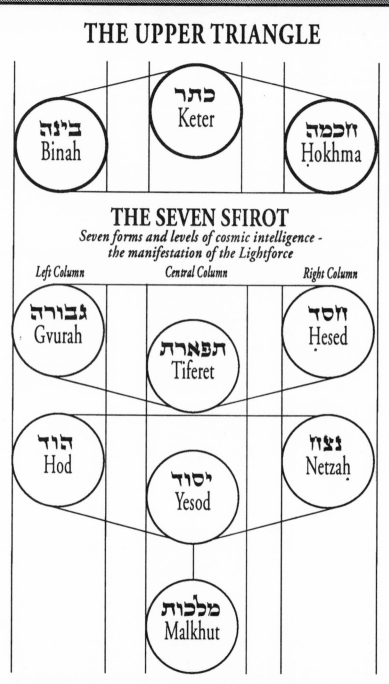

כתר
Keter

בינה
Binah

חכמה
Ḥokhma

THE SEVEN SFIROT

*Seven forms and levels of cosmic intelligence -
the manifestation of the Lightforce*

Left Column   *Central Column*   *Right Column*

גבורה
Gvurah

תפארת
Tiferet

חסד
Ḥesed

הוד
Hod

יסוד
Yesod

נצח
Netzaḥ

מלכות
Malkhut

*These intelligence-coded messages (metaphysical DNA) account for
our grand solar system and for the earth's cosmic division. The seven Sfirot
are encased in the heart and soul of the planets. The shell of each planet is
an aspect of body consciousness.*

APPENDIX 2
The Shield of David

The Shield of David, in a broader sense, implies the concept of cosmic consciousness. When a thorough knowledge of the Upper and Lower Triads has been achieved then one can reach a *Dvekut* with the cosmos which is represented by the Shield of David. Cosmic influences, namely the seven basic planets together with the twelve signs of the Zodiac, are directly related and bound up with the above seven *Sfirot*. Each *Sfirah* is considered the internal energy of the seven planets which are as follows: Saturn, Jupiter, Mars, Sun, Venus, Mercury and the Moon, in this order. Each planet rules over and dominates two signs of the Zodiac. The sun and moon rule over only one sign. Through Kabbalistic Meditation, one can connect with cosmic consciousness thereby achieving a level of pure awareness. When the individual has mastered the art of direct communion with and an attachment to the inner aspect of these cosmic influences, the *Sfirot*, then it is the individual who can now *direct* his destiny.

The Shield of David

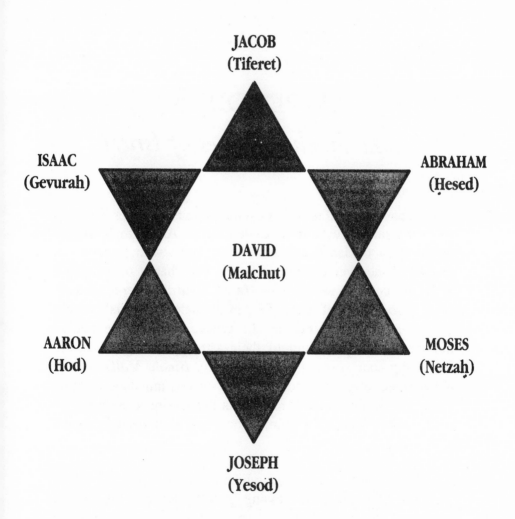

JACOB
(Tiferet)

ISAAC
(Gevurah)

ABRAHAM
(Ḥesed)

DAVID
(Malchut)

AARON
(Hod)

MOSES
(Netzaḥ)

JOSEPH
(Yesod)

APPENDIX 3
The Twelve Tribes of Israel

We have learned that Biblical narrative is the outer covering for many inner levels of concealed truths. An example of this is the story of Jacob and his twelve sons, who became the leaders of the twelve tribes of Israel. The chariot of the *sfirah* of *Tiferet* contains six *sfirot* — *Hesed, Gvurah, Tiferet, Netzah, Hod, Yesod*. Each of these *sfirot* in its male and female aspect can be attributed to one of the twelve sons, to the twelve months of the year, and to their astrological signs. Of the remaining four *sfirot (Keter, Hokhmah, Binah, Malkhut)*, the upper three have no direct influence on this mundane level of existence, while *Malkhut* represents the Desire to Receive — man himself, who is the ultimate recipient of all these energies.

The list on the next page, which is derived from the words of Torah concerning the blessing given by Jacob to his sons, is presented for the reader's interest and information. A more detailed discussion of the subject will be found in the volume *Astrology: The Star Connection.*

TRIBE	SFIRAH	MONTH
Reuben	Hesed	Nisan
Shimon	Gvurah	Iyar
Levi	Tiferet	Sivan
Yehudah	Netzah	Tammuz
Yisechar	Hod	Av
Zebulun	Yesod	Elul
Binyamin	Hesed	Tishrei
Dan	Gvurah	Marheshvan
Naftali	Tiferet	Kislev
Gad	Netzah	Tevet
Asher	Hod	Shvat
Yosef	Yesod	Adar

SIGN (Hebrew)	SIGN (English)	ZODIAC (Conventional)
Taleh	Lamb	Aries
Shor	Ox	Taurus
Te'omim	Twins	Gemini
Sartan	Crab	Cancer
Aryeh	Lion	Leo
Betulah	Virgin	Virgo
Moznaim	Scales	Libra
Akrav	Scorpion	Scorpio
Keshet	Rainbow	Sagittarius
Gdi	Goat	Capricorn
Dli	Vessel	Aquarius
Dagim	Fish	Pisces

APPENDIX 4
Biographical Notes

Aaron haLevy: (ca. 1234-1300 Barcelona) Known for his work *Sefer haHinukh* (Book of Education); Student of Nahmanides.

Aaron Berekiah ben Moses of Modena: (ca. 1600) Italian Kabbalist famous for his *Ma'avar Yabok* (Crossing the *Yabok*), one of the most profound concepts in Kabbalah.

Abarbanel, Rabbi Don Isaac: (b. Lisbon 1437, d. Venice 1509) Prediscovered the wondrous world of the mystical realm in general and the Kabbalah in particular. Served the Spanish Royal House before the expulsion of the Jews from Spain. He succeeded in piercing the iron curtain concealing the mysterious enigmas of redemption cloaked in the Book of Daniel. He offered encouragement to Jews following their expulsion from Spain by composing several works concerned with the central desire of that period, the coming of the Messiah.

Abba, Rabbi: (ca. 130 C.E.) Student of Rabbi Shimon bar Yohai who, according to the Zohar (III, P.287b) actually put into writing the words of the Zohar as they were revealed by Rabbi Shimon bar Yohai.

Abbaye: (ca. 270-339 C.E.) One of the most prominent Amoraim; together with his opponent Rava mentioned most often in discourses in the Babylonian Talmud.

Abraham: (ca. 1900 B.C.E.) Partriarch, considered to be the chariot of the *Sfirah Ḥesed* (Kindness), as exemplified in the Book of Genesis.

Abraham ben David of Posquieres, Rabbi: (ca. 1125-1198) known by his acronym RABAD. Kabbalistic and Talmudic authority who lived in Provence. A distinguished authoritative scholar known for his in-depth criticism of Maimonides, produced numerous literary works, *Torat haBayit* and *Ba'al haNefesh* to mention two. His commentary on the *Sefer Yetzirah* is of special significance, inasmuch as this work established the RABAD as one of the most prominent figures in Kabbalistic literature. This work and his probing into the metaphysical strata of Kabbalah exerted considerable influence on subsequent Spanish Kabbalists. He defined heretofore abstract concepts with a maximum of clarity. For this he attained for himself a special place in history as one of the greatest commentators on the Kabbalah.

Abraham ben Eliezer haLevy Beruchim: (ca. 1515-1593) Kabbalist born in Morocco who later settled in Safed where he joined first the school of Rabbi Moses Cordovero and then Rabbi Isaac Luria's circle.

Abraham ben Eliezer haLevi: (ca. 1450-1530) Spanish Kabbalist known for his *Masoret haHokhmah* (Transmission of the Wisdom) who after the expulsion of the Jews from Spain settled in Jerusalem.

Abraham ben Isaac: (Gerondi) (ca. 13th century) Famous Spanish Kabbalist whose Kabbalistic hymns and prayers are widely known. *Ahot Ketannah* (Little Sister) his most famous prayer recited before the Rosh HaShanah prayers describes the exile of the Jewish people, or more specifically, *Galut ha-Shekhinah*.

Abraham ben Isaac of Narbonne: (ca. 1110-1179) Talmudist and Rabbi of Provence whose famous work, *Sefer haEshkol*, was the primary work of codification of Halakha, which served as a model for subsequent codifications. Father-in-law of Abraham ben David of Posquieres, the RABAD.

Abraham ben Israel of Brody: (1749-1836) Famed Italian Kabbalist known for his extreme piety and fasting. Author of many Kabbalistic works.

Abraham ben Moses ben Maimon: (1186-1237) Son of Maimonides, scholar and subsequent leader of the Egyptian Jewish community following the death of his father. After the great controversy erupted in Provence and Spain over the writings of his father, he came to his father's defense. While Maimonides directed all his efforts to codifying the Talmud, his son's view of Judaism was of a mystical nature.

Abulafia, Abraham ben Samuel: (ca. 1240-1290) Kabbalist of Spain and Italy. He considered himself the representative of prophetic Kabbalah.

Aderet, Solomon ben Abraham: (ca. b. 1235 Barcelona, d. 1310) Also known as the RASHBA, acronym for his full name, famous for his talmudical commentaries, poetry, philosophy and lesser known for his Kabbalistic writings. Student of Rabbi Jonah Gerondi and Nahmanides.

Akiva, Rabbi ben Joseph: (ca. 15-135 C.E.) Younger contemporary of Rabbi Gamliel; teacher of Rabbi Shimon bar Yohai, the author of the Zohar (*Book of Splendor*); began the study of the Torah at the age of forty, motivated by his wife Rachel, the daughter of the wealthy Kalba Sevua by whom he was employed as a shepherd (*Tractate Ketubot*, P. 62b.). One of the most prominent leaders (*Tanna*), his disciples in his academy at Bene Berak numbered some twenty-four thousand (*Tractate Sanhedrin* 32A); he compiled and systemized the topics of *Torah Bal Peh* (Talmud) known as the Mishnah of Rabbi Akiva (*Mishnah, Tractate Sanhedrin* 3). This work laid the foundation for the final compilation of the Mishna by Rabbi Jehudah haNassi (the Prince). Main supporter of Bar Kokhba whom he considered to be the Messiah, in the latter's insurrection against Rome; captured by the Romans and put to death for studying Torah, expiring with the *Shema* upon his lips. "With the passing of Rabbi Akiva, the crown of the Torah ceased to exist" (*Tractate Sotah* 92).

Alkabetz, Rabbi Shlomo haLevi: (b. 1505 Salonica, d. 1576 Safed) Kabbalist and mystical poet, author of Lecha Dodi recited Friday evening, founder of the famous Kabbalistic centre at Salonica. He was a contemporary of Rabbi Joseph Karo, author of the Shulhan Arukh, and the Ari, Rabbi Isaac Luria.

Alsheikh, Rabbi Moses (b. 1508, d. 1600 Damascus) Most important homiletician of the 16th century, contemporary of Rabbi Joseph Karo and the Ari, Rabbi Isaac Luria. Member of the Rabbinical Council in Safed, wrote an allegorical-mystical Bible commentary.

Ari: See Luria, Rabbi Yitzhak.

Ashlag, Rabbi Yehuda: (1886-1955) Famed Kabbalist known as the pioneer of modern Kabbalism, developed a new approach to the understanding of the Lurianic system. His profound yet accessible writings provided the necessary keys in comprehending the Zohar. His translation of the entire Zohar, known as the *Sulam,* facilitated the widespread interest of this sublime and obstruse text. He opened the portals to spiritual Judaism through his sixteen volume textbook called *The Study of the Ten Luminous Emanations.*

Attar, Rabbi Haim: (b. 1696 Morocco, d. 1743 Jerusalem) Kabbalist who became famous for his best known and important commentary on the Bible, *Or haHaim* (Light of Life), based entirely on Kabbalistic teachings. In 1741, settled in Jerusalem and established an academy of learning. His yarzeit is celebrated by many thousands of Jews each year in Jerusalem.

Azulai, Rabbi Abraham Ben Mordekhai: (1570-1643) Famous Kabbalist born in Fez from a family of Kabbalists of Castilian origin, wrote three treatises on the Zohar; *Or Levanah* (Light of the Moon), *Or haHamah* (Light of the Sun), and *Or haGanuz* (the Hidden Light), based primarily on the Lurianic system. Underscored the permission granted for all to enter the gates of the world of mysticism.

Azulai, Rabbi Haim Yosef David: (b. 1724 Jerusalem, d. 1806 Leghorn) Known by his Hebrew acronym HIDA. Kabbalist, halakhist and historian, authored the famous bibliographic work Shem-HaGedolim.

Baal Shem: see Israel Baal Shem Tov

Bahya ben Asher ben Halava: (13th century) Spanish Kabbalist famous for his commentary on the Bible and numerous works on the Kabbalah, disciple of Solomon ben Abraham Aderet.

Bahya, Rabbi Ibn Pakuda: (ca. 1080-1170) Kabbalist and philosopher who lived in Spain, author of the famous work *Hovat haLevavot* (Duties of the Heart).

Barzillai, Judah ben Al-Bargeloni: (12th century) Spanish Kabbalist and halachist known for his commentary on the *Sefer Yetzirah* called *Perush Sefer Yetzirah*. His other works include *Sefer haIttim*, which deals with the Jewish festivals which are referred to extensively by later commentaries.

Ben Azzai: (ca. 130 C.E.) A younger contemporary of Rabbi Akiba. The Talmud and Zohar say Four persons entered the Pardes (Orchard), concerning the nature and process of creation. These were: Ben Azzai, Ben Zoma, Aher (another, the surname given to Elisha Ben Abuyah) and Rabbi Akiba. Ben Azzai, Ben Zoma and Aher entered the domains of *p'shat* (simple), *remez* (hint), *drush* (homiletical) interpretations of the Torah. Rabbi Akiba entered the domain of *Sod* (Kabbalah) and he alone survived. (Zohar I,P.26b and tractate Hagigah,P.14b). Ben Zoma said, "Who is wise? He who learns from all men, as it is written: From all my teachers have I gained knowledge." (Psalms 119:99).

Ben HaKanah: see Nehemia ben HaKanah

Ben Zakai: see Johanan ben Zakai

Besht: see Israel Baal Shem Tov

Botarel, Moses ben Isaac: (15th century) Spanish Kabbalist, whose main work is a commentary on the *Sefer Yetzirah*. This invaluable work stemmed from his desire to enhance the status of Kabbalism.

Brandwein, Rabbi Yehuda Zvi: (1904-1969) Kabbalist and significant student of Rabbi Ashlag. His vast knowledge of the Lurianic system enabled him to codify and edit the entire writings of the Ari, Rabbi Isaac Luria. Continued with the similar style of translation and commentary of Rabbi Ashlag known as *Ma'alot haSulam* (Extension of the Ladder) on those works of Rabbi Shimon bar Yohai, which Rabbi Ashlag was not able to complete during his lifetime, namely *Hashmatot haZohar* (Various other Writings) and *Tikune Zohar* (Addendum to the Zohar). First Jewish settler within the Old City of Jerusalem after the Six day War.

Cordovero, Rabbi Moses: (1522-1570) Also known by the abbreviation REMAK, famed Kabbalist of Safed's "golden age", brother in law of Rabbi Shlomo Alkabetz, and one-time teacher of the Ari, Rabbi Isaac Luria. His large main work *Or Yakar*, (Precious Light), on the entire Zohar has only recently begun to see the light of day. Originator of one of the two basic systems of understanding the Zohar. His other major work *Pardes Rimmonim* (Garden of Pomegranates) is a systematic compendium of Kabbalistic concepts surrounding the internal action of the original unified energy force emanating from the Creator. Rabbi Haim Vital, student of Rabbi Isaac Luria, had a dream in which the Remak revealed to him that in the age of the Messiah the Lurianic system would prevail.

Crescas, Hasdai: (b. 1340 Barcelona, d. 1412 Zaragoza) Famed Spanish Kabbalist and philosopher whose criticism of Jewish Aristotelianism provided a stimulus for and paved the way to an in-depth recognition of the internal, metaphysical world of reality. His main work was *Or Adonai* (The Light of G-d) in which he presented his criticism of Jewish Aristotelianism.

De Leon, Moses ben Shem Tov: (1250 Guadalajara, 1305 Avila) Famed Kabbalist in Spain who revealed for the first time the existence of a physical instrument that can provide spiritual insights into the five books of Moses — the Zohar, (*Book of Splendor*) — the main work of Kabbalistic literature.

Donolo Shabbatai: (c. 913-982) Famed Italian Kabbalist and physician who was born in Oria, Italy. His most famous work on Kabbalah is his book *Sefer Hakhmoni*, a commentary on the *Sefer Yetzirah*. His *Sefer haMirkahot* (Book of Remedies) drew material from his knowledge of *Hakarot haPartzuf* (physiognomies) and astrology, which undoubtedly was based on his comprehension of the Kabbalah. His *Sefer Hakhmoni* provides a massive collection of information regarding the study of astronomy; without it, the study of astrology would remain incomprehensible.

Eleazar ben Judah: Rabbi of Worms (ca. 1176 Speyer, d. 1238 Worms) Student of Rabbi Judah ben Samuel, the Pious. His work *Rokeah* presents a concept of mysticism relating to moral practice.

Elijah ben Solomon: see the "Gaon of Vilna"

Elisha ben Abuyah: (2nd century) Entered the Pardes and became heretical, known as Aher ("that other one").

Galante, Rabbi Abraham: (ca. 1570) Famed Safed Kabbalist of the sixteenth century, known for his commentary on the Zohar.

Galico, Rabbi Elisha: (16th century) Famed Kabbalist known for his commentary on the Zohar. Member of the Rabbinical Court of Rabbi Yosef Karo in Safed.

Gaon of Vilna: (1720-1797) HaGaon Rabbi Eliyahu (abreviated HAGRA), famous for his Kabbalistic writings which number some eighty volumes, halakhist of the Talmud.

Gerondi, Rabbi Moses ben Solomon d'Escola: (b. 1244 Gerona, d. 1263 Toledo) Cousin of Nahmanides, famous for ethical writings, *Sha'arei Teshuvah* and *Sefer haYira*.

Gikatila, Rabbi Joseph: (ca.1270) Famed Spanish Kabbalist whose writings, *Ginat Egoz* (Garden of Nut Trees), *Igeret haKodesh* (Holy Letter) and *Sha'arei Orah* (Gates of Light), provided a systematic development to the internal structure and meaning of symbolism.

Haim, Rabbi Kohen: (ca. 1600) Famed Kabbalist of Aleppo, student of Rabbi Haim Vital, composer of mystical hymns in the form of dialogues between the Creator and Israel.

Haim Vital, Rabbi: (b.1543 Safed, d. 1620 Damascus) Selected student of Rabbi Isaac Luria, the Ari, who together with his son Shmuel accepted the task of recording the Ari's thoughts on paper.

Hida: see Azulai, Rabbi Haim Yosef David

Ibn Gaon, Shem Tov ben Abraham: (late 13th to 14th centuries) Spanish Kabbalist and halakhist whose teacher was Solomon ben Abraham Aderet. His best known work on the Kabbalah is *Keter Shem Tov* and *Migdal Oz*, a commentary on the *Mishneh Torah* of Maimonides.

Ibn Habib, Jacob ben Solomon: (ca. 1440-1515) Rabbinical scholar born in Castile, Spain. Heading a *yeshivah* which was one of the largest in Spain. On the expulsion of the Jews from Spain he went to Portugal and then on to Salonika, which had become the main center for the study of Kabbalah. His most famous work *Ein Ya'akov*, in which he assembled the *Agadot* of the Babylonian and Jerusalem Talmud.

Ibn Motot, Samuel ben Saadiah: (ca. 1370) Spanish Kabbalist and was one of the inner circle of Spanish Kabbalists in Castile.

Ibn Shem Tov, Shem Tov: (ca. 1380-1440) Spanish Kabbalist, known as the anti-Maimonidean Kabbalist.

Ibn Waqar, Joseph ben Abraham: (ca. 14th century) Kabbalist who lived in Toledo, Spain and formulated his Kabbalistic ideas through his now famous poem, *Shir haYihud.*

Isaac ben Todros of Barcelona: (14th century) Spanish Kabbalist and student of Nahmanides whose teachings are included among the writings of the disciples of Nahmanides.

Isaac the Blind: (ca. 1200) Famous Spanish Kabbalist who lived in Provence. Son of the famed Kabbalist, Rabbi Abraham ben David of Posquieres.

Isaiah ben Abraham Horowitz, Rabbi: (1565-1630) Kabbalist, author of *Shnei Luhot haBrit* (The two Tablets of the Covenant) also known by the acronym SHALOH.

Ishmael, Rabbi ben Elisha: (b. ?, d. 135 C.E.) Famous Tanna and contemporary of Rabbi Akiba who was among the martyrs of the Hadrian persecution in 135 C.E. He won for himself a permanent place as a figure in Jewish mysticism with his explanations of the twenty-two letters of the Hebrew alphabet as described in his *Baraita de Rabbi Ishmael.* He also authored *Thirteen Principles of Logic.*

Israel Baal Shem Tov: (1700-1760) Also known as BESHT (abbreviation of Baal Shem Tov). The founder of Ḥasidism. The light of his teaching and his holy wisdom is based on the foundations of the Ari, Rabbi Isaac Luria. The BESHT passed on his teachings only by word of mouth. However, the internal strength of his teachings represented for the average Jew of Eastern Europe the opportunity of reaching endless heights of spiritual development with the help of Kabbalistic *Kavannot.* "The act of *dvekut*," (union with the light), remarked the BESHT, "can best be achieved by man through joy and the proper relationship to his fellow man, and that the Creator, the source of internal energy and strength dwell within us at all times, and what is left to man is to reveal and activate this potential energy."

Jacob ben Jacob, haKohen: (ca. 13th century) Famed Kabbalist of the communities in Provence and Spain. Various works on Kabbalah have been attributed to him, however, without certainty.

Johanan (Yohanan) ben Zakai, Rabbi: (ca. 50 C.E.) Youngest disciple of Hillel who foresaw the destruction of the

Temple (*Tractate Yuma* 39b), concluded that the establishment of a Torah center was the last and only hope for the Jews to exist as a nation without the binding force of the Holy Temple. Was smuggled out of Jerusalem as a corpse by his students Rabbi Eliezer ben Hyrcanus and Rabbi Joshua ben Hananiah, and presented himself before the Roman commander Vespasian asking his permission to establish a Torah academy in Yavneh. (*Tractate Gitin* 55b.) His request granted, Yavneh became the spiritual center of Jewish life where the Great Sanhedrin was reestablished.

Joseph Ibn Shraga: (15th century) Famed Italian Kabbalist.

Joseph Ibn Tabul: (ca. 16th century) Kabbalist who lived in Safed and taught the Lurianic system of Kabbalah.

Judah ben Kalonymus ben Moses of Mainz: (13th century) Kabbalist and halakhic authority whose teacher in mysticism was Judah ben Samuel haHasid.

Judah ben Samuel haHasid: (ca.1150-1217) Kabbalist who lived in Regensburg. Although known for his work *Sefer Hasidim*, he was the teacher of many subsequent Kabbalists among whom were his grandson, Eleazar ben Moses haDarshon, and his great grandson, Moses ben Eleazar.

Karo, Rabbi Joseph: (b. 1488 Spain, d. 1575 Safed) Author of the *Shulhan Arukh* the most authoritative codification of Jewish law, and great Rabbinical authority of the sixteenth century. Also known for his Kabbalistic writing *Magid Mesharim* which contains visions and revelations only attributable to a Kabbalist.

Levi, Rabbi Isaac of Berdichev: (1740-1809) Famous Hasidic Master whose constant use of the expression "Derbarmdiger Gott" (Merciful Lord), he was known as the "Derbarmdiger" for his principles: love of the Lord and love of your fellow man.

Loew, Rabbi Judah ben Bezalel: (1525-1609) The Great Rabbi Loew, abbreviated as MAHARAL, had earned a reputation as a performer of miracles and famed for his Kabbalistic writings: *Be'er haGolah*, *Netivot Olam*, and *Tiferet Israel*.

Luria, Rabbi Isaac: (b. 1534 Jerusalem, d. 1572 Safed) Known as the "Ari", the "Lion" or "Ari haKadosh", the Holy Lion, founder of the Lurianic system of Kabbalah.

Luzzatto, Rabbi Moshe Haim: (b. 1707 Padua, d. 1746 Tiberias) Also known by the acronym RAMHAL. Kabbalist and Poet, author of the Book, *The One Hundred Thirty Eight Openings to the Kabbalah* and his ethical religious work, *Mesillat Yesharim* (Paths of the Upright).

Maharal: see Loew, Rabbi Judah ben Bezalal

Maimonides, Rabbi Moses Ben Maimon: (b. 1135 Cordoba, d. 1204 Fostat; buried in Tiberias) Known by the Acronym RAMBAM. Born in Cordova, Spain, Maimonides was forced to emigrate, at first to Morocco, then to Egypt where he earned his living practicing medicine. His *Mishnah Torah* (Copy of the Law) was the first systematic exposition of Jewish Law. His "articles of faith", are quoted in most Jewish prayer books. Most important Jewish philosopher of the Middle ages. His thoughts strongly influenced all philosophical thinking of his era through his main philosophical work *Moreh Nevokhim* (Guide for the Perplexed). Also *Yad haHazakah* (Strong Hand) is a restructuring of the whole content of Biblical Law.

Meir (Enlightener): (2nd century C.E.) *Tanna* and one of the most prominent disciples of Rabbi Akiba. One of the five surviving students who did not perish in the great plague of Roman bestiality and the death of Rabbi Akiba's 24,000 students. His work in systemizing the Halakhah, laid the foundation of the present Mishnah. He was the husband of the famous Beruria, daughter of the martyred Rabbi Hananiah ben Tradion.

Menaḥem Azariah of Fano: (ca. 1609) Famous Italian Kabbalist whose work *Maamar haNefesh* follows the mystical idea developed by Rabbi Isaac Luria concerning the soul, in that each letter of the Torah represents the upper root of the soul of each individual in Israel. Consequently, each individual soul has its own framework of reference in understanding the Torah.

Moses, Rabbi ben Jacob: (ca.1440-1520) Talmudic scholar and Kabbalist who lived in Lithuania. Famous for his commentary *Otzar haShem* on the *Sefer Yetzirah* and *Shushan Sodot* dealing with cryptic writing.

Moses ben Maimon: See Maimonides

Moses ben Nahman: See Naḥmanides

Moses ben Shem Tov de Leon: see De Leon

Moses, Rabbi ben Solomon of Burgos: (ca. 1230-1300) A leading Kabbalist in Spain, student of Jacob ben Jacob haKohen of Provence.

Naḥmanides, Rabbi Moses ben Naḥman: (1194 Gerona, d. 1270 Akko) abbreviated RAMBAN. Famed Spanish Kabbalist, Talmudic scholar and biblical exegete who adopted a mystical position in the battle which raged around philosophy during the thirteenth century. His commentary on the *Sefer Yetzirah* provides an in-depth comprehension to this abstruse and difficult work on the Kabbalah. His commentary on the Bible cannot be understood apart from a comprehension of the Kabbalah. His opposition to Aristotelianism, which had endangered the very foundations of Judaism in Spain, was based completely on the principal doctrines of the Zohar, which legend relates was already known to Nahmanides. The mysteries of the Kabbalah which initially took hold during the latter half of the twelfth century in Provence and subsequently came to full bloom there and in Northern Spain in the thirteenth century was the Creator's beneficence for a reawakening and rebirth of a new life under its influence. Nahmanides played no small role in this new development if not possibly the harbinger of this movement which climaxed a period in the history of the Jews on which they have always looked back with pride when referring to this "Golden Age in Spain".

Najara, Rabbi Moses: (ca. 16th century) Kabbalist who lived in Safed and studied within the school of the Lurianic system. Author of several works on the Kabbalah.

Nathan haBavli, Rabbi: (ca. 170 C.E.) An older contemporary of Rabbi Judah haNassi of the Talmudic period, author of a parallel work to the Tractate *Ethics of the Fathers* which is a homiletical exposition of *Pirkei Avot*.

Nehemia ben HaKanah, Rabbi: (ca. 70-130 C.E.) A student of Rabbi Johanan ben Zakkai (*Baba Batra* 10a). A famed mystic and author of *Ana BeKoah* a recitation included in the morning and afternoon prayers. This profound mystical prayer is connected with and related to the Seven *Sefirot* inasmuch as each of the seven sentences relate to a particular *Sfirah*. This prayer is also included in the counting of the *Omer* with its significance being the mystical relationship to each day of the forty-nine days that commence with the second day of Passover and end the day before *Shavuot*. Since the cosmological influence during this period is considered to be totally negative and destructive, the Ari, Rabbi Isaac Luria, explains in his *Book of Meditation*, the use of this prayer to alter the Cosmic influence of these forty-nine days. He has also been considered the author of the famed Kabbalistic text, the *Sefer Bahir*.

Obadiah ben Abraham Bertinoro: (b. ca. 1430 Italy, d. 1525 Jerusalem) Famous for his commentary on the Mishnah.

Pinhas ben Yair: *Tannah* of the first Century and father in law of Rabbi Shimon bar Yohai.

Poppers, Meir ben Judah Loeb haKohen: (17th century) Kabbalist, student of Jacob Zemah and one of the final editors of Haim Vital's writings of the *Kitvei haAri* (writings of the Ari). He wrote extensively according to the Lurianic system.

Rabad: see Abraham ben David of Posquieres

Radbaz: see Zimra, David ben

Rambam: see Maimonides

Ramban: see Nahmanides

Rashba: see Aderet, Solomon ben Abraham

Recanati, Rabbi Menahem ben Benyamin: (ca. 1350-1440) Italian Kabbalist, whose family originally came from Spain. His main Kabbalistic work was *Perush Ol haTorah* (commentary on

the Torah), and *Ta'amei haMitzvot* (Explanation of the precepts). He is quoted extensively throughout the writings of the
Ari, Rabbi Isaac Luria. The Ari, mentioning *The Sefer haReca-
nati*, tells of an incident where a person, who, on the night of
Hoshana Rabba — which according to the Zohar, is the time
when we can know if our sins have been purified and we shall
live for another year — went out at midnight according to the
teachings of the Ari. Upon seeing that his full shadow didn't
appear and the head was missing, he knew this was a sign that
he needed to attain a higher degree of purity. He returned to the
house of study and wept and repented wholeheartedly and when
he felt cleaner inside he went outside again and observed that
his prayers had been accepted as he saw his full shadow by the
light of the moon. (*Gate of Meditation*, p.307b)

Saadia ben Joseph Gaon: (882-942 C.E.) Born in Egypt,
author, scholar, Kabbalist of the gaonic period and leader of
Babylonian Jewry. His original commentary on the *Sefer
Yetzirah* was written in Arabic and translated into Hebrew. His
principal work was *Emunot veDe'ot* (Doctrines and Opinions).

Saba, Abraham ben Jacob: (ca. 1500) Spanish Kabbalist and
exegete, who settled in Portugal after the expulsion of the Jews
from Spain. When forced conversion of Jews was decreed in
Portugal in 1497, he left for Fez in Morocco. Known for his
famed work on the Bible, *Tsror haMor*, and *Perush Eser
haSfirot* (Explanation of the Ten Sfirot).

Sahula, Isaac ben Solomon Abi: (ca. 1240) Scholar and
Kabbalist who lived in the town of Guadalajara in Castile. Was
a student of the famed Kabbalist Moses of Burgos and acquain-
tance of Moses ben Shem Tov de Leon.

Sahula, Meir ben Solomon Abi: (ca. 1250-1335), Spanish Kabbalist and younger brother of Isaac Abi Sahula who lived in Guadalajara which was then a center of Kabbalistic learning. Famous for his commentary of the *Sefer Yetzirah* and *Sefer haBahir*.

Shmuel Vital: (ca. 1598-1678), Kabbalist, son of Haim Vital, considered among the important Talmudic authorities of Damascus, reedited his fathers writings which the Ari, Rabbi Isaac Luria, transmitted orally.

Sharabi, Shalom: (1720-1777) Kabbalist born in Yemen, emigrated to Palestine and studied at the Kabbalistic Yeshivah Bet El in Jerusalem. As a Jerusalem Kabbalist, he studied the Lurianic system of Kabbalah. His works are on Lurianic Kabbalah. Particularly famous is his *Nehar Shalom*, which includes the secrets and meditations on prayer and *mitzvot*.

Shaloh: see Isaiah ben Abraham Horowitz

Shimon haTsadik: Member of the Sanhedrin and High Priest of the Second temple.

Solomon Aderet: see Aderet, Solomon

Vital: see Haim Vital

Vital, Joseph: (15th century) Scribe, especially known for his preciseness in writing tefillin which were known as Tefillin of the Rabbi of Calabria. Father of Haim Vital.

Vital, Moses ben Joseph: Younger brother of Haim Vital and active in the Kabbalistic circle of Safed.

Vital, Shmuel: see Shmuel Vital

Yosi ben Jacob: One of the ten students of Rabbi Shimon bar Yohai who left his body during the Greater Assembly.

Zacuto, Moses ben Mordekhai: (ca. 1620-1697) Kabbalist and poet. He was born into a Portuguese Marrano family in Amsterdam. Zacuto published exoteric works in addition to his numerous writings on the Kabbalah.

Zemah, Jacob ben Haim: (17th century) Famed Kabbalist born in Portugal, settled in Safed where he took up the study of Kabbalah in the Lurianic tradition. Author of many works on the Zohar as well as Lurianic concepts and customs.

Zimra, David ben: (b. 1479 Spain, d. 1573 Safed) Known as the RADBAZ. He was exiled from Spain at age 13 and moved to Safed. In 1512 went to Egypt where he became spiritual leader until 1569 when he returned to Safed. His distinguished student during his stay in Egypt was the Ari, Rabbi Isaac Luria.

REFERENCES

PART ONE — THE BODY OF KNOWLEDGE

Chapter 1: THE MAIN TEACHINGS

1. Etz Haim, Gate I, Branch II. cf. Ten Luminous Emanations, Vol. 1, p.33, Jerusalem 1972, Research Centre of Kabbalah.
2. Talmud Eser Sfirot, Vol. 1, p.6, Hebrew 1956, Research Centre. This same idea is expressed in the Ten Luminous Emanations, Vol. I.
3. Ibid. p.67.
4. Ibid. p.67.

Chapter 2: METHODOLOGY OF KABBALAH

5. Autobiography p.127. (Max Planck)
6. Deut, ch. 12:23
7. Zohar III, p.152a.
8. Zohar III, p.99b.

Chapter 3: THE MAJOR CONCEPTS

9. Zohar I, p.164a.
10. Sefer Hakdamot, p.52, Research Centre 1978
11. Isaiah, ch. 6:3.

12. Ten Luminous Emanations, Vol. 1, Research Centre 1978.
13. Genesis 2:5
14. Ibid. 3:17
15. Ibid. 4:12
16. Ibid. 3:18
17. Zohar I p.97a
18. Genesis 3:19
19. Zohar I p.134b.
20. Genesis 18:1.
21. Genesis 25:28.
22. Ibid. 25:27
23. Ibid. 32:29
24. Exodus, 17:11.
25. Midrash Rabba, Chukkas.
26. Tractate M'Nahoth, p.29b, Talmud Bavli, cf. Gates of Reincarnation, p.103, Jerusalem 1978, Research Centre.
27. Midrash Rabbah, Vayhi.
28. Tractate M'Nahoth, p.29b, Talmud Bavli.
29. Deut. 4:4.
30. Zohar III, Idra Rabba, p.143a.
31. Gate of Reincarnation, p.79, Vol. 13, 1978 Jerusalem, Research Centre.
32. Exodus, 2:2.
33. Gate of Reincarnation, p.97, Vol. 13, 1978 Jerusalem, Research Centre.
34. Tractate Pesachim, p.49b,Talmud Bavli.
35. Zohar III, p.151b.
36. Genesis, 41:56. cf. Zohar I. p.197a.
37. Zohar Hadash, p.67c.
38. Ten Luminous Emanations, Vol I, p.55-76, Jerusalem 1978, Research Centre.
39. Ibid. p.74.
40. Zohar I, p.34a.
41. Zohar I, p.18a.
42. Ten Luminous Emanations, Vol. 1, Jerusalem 1978, Research Centre.
43. Zohar II, P.176a.
44. Malahai 3:6.
45. Zohar I, p.15a.
46. Zohar Hadash, Song of Songs p.70 sec 5..

PART TWO — ORIGINS AND HISTORY

Chapter 4: KABBALAH — A DEFINITION

47. Ethics of the Fathers, I:1.
48. Tractate Tamid, p.32a, Talmud Bavli.

Chapter 5: THE ORIGINS OF THE KABBALAH

49. Tractate Berakhot, 20a, Talmud Bavli.
50. Tikune Zohar, p.1a, Zohar Hadash, p.59.
51. Likutai Torah, p.126, Vol. 12, 1970 Jerusalem, Research Centre of Kabbalah.
52. Gate of Reincarnation, p.113, Vol. 13, 1970 Jerusalem, Research Centre of Kabbalah.
53. Zohar III, p.100b.
54. Gate of the Parables of Rashbi, Vol.6, p.91, Tel Aviv, 1969, Research Centre of Kabbalah.
55. Exodus 10:1.
56. Zohar II, p.34a.
57. Deut. 32:39.
58. Zohar I, p.22b.

Chapter 6: RABBI SHIMON BAR YOHAI AND THE
                GREATER ASSEMBLY

59. Zohar I, p.11a.
60. Rabbis Abba, Yehuda, Yosi ben Jacob, Yitzhak, Hezekiah ben Rav, Chiya, Yosi and Yisa.
61. Zohar III, Idra Rabba, p.127b.
62. Zohar III, Idra Rabba, p.144a.
63. Zohar III, Idra Rabba p.144a.
64. Zohar Khadash, Vayyera p.26b.
65. Zohar I, p.24a, cf. Ashlag ed.
66. Ibid. p.174b.
67. Zohar III, Deuteronomy, p.287b.

Chapter 7: THE GOLDEN AGE OF SAFED

68. Isaiah, 2:3.
69. Exodus, 34:23.
70. Ibid 21:2.
71. Gate of Reincarnation, p.133, Jerusalem, 1978, Research Centre.
72. Ibid. p.129.
73. Ibid. p.135.
74. Ibid. p.135.
75. Ibid. p.136.
76. Ibid. p.136.
77. Ibid. p.138.
78. Ibid. p.138.
79. Ibid. p.156
80. Ibid. p.156.
81. Ibid. p.139.
82. Ibid. p.148.

Chapter 8: A LATER LIGHT — RABBI ASHLAG

83. For full text, see Entrance to the Zohar, Philip S. Berg, Jerusalem 1974, Research Centre of Kabbalah, p.7.

PART THREE — MAKING THE CONNECTION —
PRACTICAL APPLICATIONS

Chapter 10: OPERATIONAL TOOLS

84. Rabbi Isaac Luria Sefer Likutei Torah V'Ta'amai haMitzvot, Jerusalem 1970, Research Centre, p.34.
85. Tractate Shabbat, p.31a.
86. Genesis, 8:21.

Chapter 11: DVEKUT: THE CIRCULAR CONCEPT

87. Tractate Kiddushim, p.2a.
88. Ibid., p.7a.
89. Ibid., p.5b.

Chapter 12: A CONTEMPLATION

90. Zohar I, p.50b.

INDEX